Sound and music   73

Imagination and drama   83

Music   92

Acknowledgements
Many thanks to Anita Lake, Louisa Oakley and Rita Thompson, not only for their ideas but also for the pleasure of working with them over the years.

And thanks too, to Ale and Hilary for all their personal support.

Action Rhymes & Games

Max de Bóo

Bright Ideas
FOR Early Years

Published by Scholastic Publications Ltd,
Villiers House, Clarendon Avenue,
Leamington Spa, Warwickshire
CV32 5PR

© 1992 Scholastic Publications Ltd
    Reprinted 1992

Written by Max de Bóo
Edited by Catherine Baker
Sub-edited by Jo Saxelby
Designed by Anna Oliwa
Illustrations by Pat Murray (Graham
Cameron Illustration)
Photographs by Peter Corbett
Cover photography by Martyn Chillmaid

Artwork by Steve Williams
& Associates, Leicester
Printed by Loxley Brothers, Sheffield

British Library Cataloguing in Publication Data
A catalogue record for this book is available from the British
Library.

ISBN 0-590-53019-4

Contents

Introduction

We live in an age of accountability, and any book for teachers of young children can be asked to justify its philosophy and the activities it recommends. I personally have no doubt of the educational validity of playing the games in this book – they can be a powerful tool for productive learning, as well as forming a link with traditions and children around the world.

The title of this book reflects my own educational bias.

Action: I want the children to *do* as much as they can, as I believe that children are at their best when they are active participants in their own learning.

Rhymes: Mastering language is a life skill, and one to be enjoyed to the full. Rhymes will long continue to capture children's interest, whether as poetry, songs or advertising jingles!

Games: Playfulness is a characteristic associated with children, and with all healthy-minded adults who retain that wonderful childlike quality.

The value of structured play

The games in this book involve structured play. However, all kinds of play have value. Spontaneous play may be initiated by children with each other:

Emma: I'll be the Mummy and you be the baby.
Tony: Yeah. Wah! Wah! Wah!

Another form of spontaneous play is initiated by children with the teacher:

Teacher: Look at these candles. Would you like to tell me about them?
Shameek: No. (Pause – giggles) And . . . (his voice drops to a whisper), if I talk like this you won't be able to hear me afterwards (on the tape recorder).

Structured play is initiated by the teacher:

Teacher: Let's play 'The farmer's in his den'. Sharon, you be the farmer . . .

Playing structured games can:
- provide a familiar and relevant yet challenging situation without prompting anxieties;
- offer a secure framework in which confidence and self-esteem can grow and different abilities are valued;
- offer opportunities for children from different backgrounds and cultures to participate verbally and non-verbally;
- provide opportunities to make mistakes in a safe setting, to take the initiative, to listen to others;
- use the children's interest as a starting point to guide them towards particular educational goals;
- offer opportunities to reinforce knowledge, understanding and skills in language, numeracy, science and drama;
- develop social and motor skills;
- develop the imagination.

Using the activities

Objectives

The chapter introductions and the stated objectives for each activity indicate some aspects of the curriculum and of development which may be emphasised in certain rhymes or games, but these are neither comprehensive nor exclusive. Most of the games will use language, motor and other skills, and many involve reasoning, sequencing and consequences.

Group size

This will depend on your circumstances. I hope that with groups of the youngest children the adult-to-child ratio will be sufficient to allow you to play all these games (in other words, two adults to twenty children). However, I know that reality is often different. What you do will be the result of a professional decision based on the amount of space you have, the number, age, experience and confidence of your children, and how much adult support you can rely on.

Resources

Generally speaking, the need for resources is slight, except where the games are followed up in other curricular areas. Hands, bodies and voices are the chief resources for the activities.

With active games space is required, perhaps on a mat or in an even larger designated area if the group is a large one. Ring games can have a positive effect on children, particularly those who are easily distracted. The eye-contact with the teacher and with each other makes participation and control easier. Try to create the space for active games if you can.

Music

It can be difficult to pitch songs at the right level for young children, and adult embarrassment together with too little singing before they come to school can create classroom 'groaners', growling in their boots. If you have a musical instrument or a chime bar, pitch the song using the octave from D above middle C, to top D or E. If you have no instrument, think of a note, then think of a *higher* one! Without a musical prop, most of us pitch tunes too low for young children. They shouldn't be asked to sing below middle C. If the children still sing low, say 'Higher!' Although some of them will confuse 'louder' with 'higher', persist. In my experience most developing 'groaners' can be diverted successfully if helped early on, and may end up singing in harmony with everyone else!

To help you further, the tunes for the less well-known action songs are set at the back of the book.

When and how?

Most of the games can be used at any time at the teacher's discretion, although there are occasional recommended times for certain games. Try to play games frequently, both at specific times and on an *ad hoc* basis during those interminable moments when waiting for someone to come or something to happen. Fill in the space with a game — it is much more fun and usually more successful than repeated requests for 'Quiet!'

Getting the pace right will depend on the children. Try not to underestimate how valuable extra time, help and examples can be, and don't forget how beneficial repetition is (this side of *ad nauseam*!). Practice reinforces familiarity, confidence, skills and understanding.

Assessment

It is possible to evaluate the effectiveness of action rhymes and games by observing some of the following:
- the degree of involvement of the children;
- the responses of the children to each other, to you and to the whole group;
- the development of confidence and self-esteem;
- the development of co-operation, sharing and tolerance of other people's points of view;
- the development of individuals' acceptance of constraints and the rules of the game, and their ability to cope with competition;
- the development of self-control and responsibility;
- the outcome in terms of discussion, the application of an activity to other curricular areas, and the children's ability to play increasingly complex games.

Links with home

By the time children come to a nursery or mainstream school, most of them will have had experience of action rhymes and games, no matter which background they come from. Following up their home experiences can reassure the children and form an important link between home and school. It can help to extend their horizons too, so that the children learn to value the co-operation of others in a larger group than the family. In games, the interaction between children and adults increases the shared enjoyment, with the children at ease and the adults confident that there is real value in rhymes and games.

Myself and other people

Chapter one

The question of greatest magnitude to follow the infant's 'What is me/not me?' is 'Who am I?' This question leads children to explore their identity, considering what their bodies are like and what they can do, what feelings they have, what likes and dislikes, how they can express themselves, what they are able and allowed to do, and what is under *their* control. We discover who we are not only by self-exploration but also by seeing our similarities with other people, how they impinge on us and affect our lives. Thus children come to understand that each of us is of value intrinsically and as a member of the group.

Pass the smile

Objective

To heighten children's awareness of feelings.

What you need

No special equipment.

What to do

This is a good game to start or finish the day, or just to establish a change of mood on a difficult day.

Sit in a ring. One person turns to the next and smiles, and that person turns to her neighbour and smiles at him, and so on until the smile has gone right around the circle.

Then pass a sad face, and a cross face. Finish off by passing a very big smile.

Follow-up

● Sing 'If you're happy and you know it'.
● Encourage the children to draw or paint some faces that are happy, sad and cross. Can they see which parts of the faces tell us what they are feeling?

I spy

Objective

To encourage self-awareness.

What you need

No special equipment.

What to do

Choose one of the children, and describe an aspect of their appearance, for example: 'I spy with my little eye, someone wearing . . . red shorts. Guess who!'

If the children have difficulty in identifying who you mean, add further descriptions, such as 'someone with red shorts and black hair', 'someone with red shorts, black hair and a blue T-shirt'.

Once the children have the idea, they can take turns to choose someone to identify.

Follow-up

If the children are beginning to develop phonic awareness, play the game in the usual way, giving the initial letter as the clue to the object you are thinking of. Give lots of examples before using each letter, for example, book, box, bottle, bear. This will help the children home in on the first sound.

What can I do with both my hands?

Objective

To help initiate younger children into joining in.

What you need

No special equipment.

What to do

Sing the following rhyme to the tune of 'The Drunken Sailor'. The children could sit or stand. Show the children how to do the actions as they sing:

> What can I do with both my hands?
> What can I do with both my hands?
> What can I do with both my hands
> Early in the morning?
>
> Give a little clap and shake them all
>   over (× 3)
> Early in the morning.
>
> What can I do with both my feet? (× 3)
> Early in the morning?
>
> Give a little stamp and shake them all
>   over (× 3)
> Early in the morning.
>
> What can I do with my whole body?
>   (× 3)
> Early in the morning?
>
> Give a little wriggle and shake it all
>   over (× 3)
> Early in the morning.

Follow-up

Continue with some more simple games and finger play.

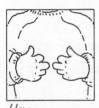

How
Knock second knuckles of two clawed hands together twice.

Well
Thumbs move down upper chest and then twist forward.

You
Point to person addressed.

Good
Thumb held up.

I
Point to self.

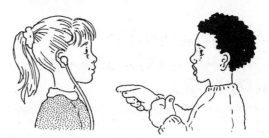

Good morning

Objective

To increase children's self-esteem.

What you need

No special equipment.

What to do

In this game, all the children sit in a circle so they can see and value each other, and each child is addressed individually. This game is especially good for children with hearing or other disabilities. Signing can be included with the questions and responses:

> 'Good morning, Jonathan. How are
>   you today?'
> 'Very well, thank you. I'm very well
>   today.'
>
> 'Good morning, Carlie. How are you
>   today?'
> 'Very well, thank you. I'm very well
>   today.'

As you say this rhyme, make the signs for some of the words as shown, mouthing the words clearly at the same time. This activity gives hearing children a chance to learn some signing too!

Follow-up

Perhaps one of the children or one of their family wears a hearing aid and could come in to show the children and talk about it.

These are Grandmother's glasses

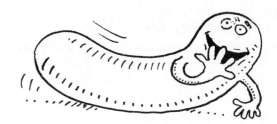

Objective

A simple game for younger children to help them become quiet.

What you need

No special equipment.

What to do

Say the following rhyme with the children:

These are Grandmother's glasses
[make circles with thumbs and forefingers]
And this is Grandmother's hat
[hands on head]
And this is the way she claps her hands
And lays them in her lap.

These are Grandfather's glasses
[make circles with thumbs and forefingers]
And this is Grandfather's hat
[hands on head]
And this is the way he folds his arms
[arms folded, chin dropped on chest]
And has a little nap.
[snore gently or stay silent]

Follow-up

• Do any of the children wear glasses, or have they had an eye-test? Talk about what happens. Do members of their family wear glasses? Why?
• Get some lenses, both convex and concave if possible, and set up a 'looking table' with some objects to inspect.

Sausages

Objective

To enable the children to have fun, while learning a little self-control.

What you need

No special equipment.

What to do

This games relies on the fact that saying 'sausages' seems to make people laugh.
 Choose one of the more confident children to begin with, and bombard her with questions, to which she may only answer, 'Sausages!' For example:
'What's your name?'
'Sausages!'
'Where do you live?'
'Sausages!'
 If the child smiles or laughs, someone replaces her and the game begins again.

Follow-up

Read some nonsense rhymes and poems, by authors such as Edward Lear, A. A. Milne, Alfred Noyes and Lewis Carroll. There are many good nonsense poetry collections, including *The Argo Book of Nonsense* (Argo, 1987); *Don't Put Mustard in the Custard* by Michael Rosen and Quentin Blake (André Deutsch, 1985); and *The Pop-up Book of Nonsense Verses* by Tony Ross (Viking Kestrel, 1989).

Eight big fingers

Objective

To help children identify the parts of the body.

What you need

No special equipment.

What to do

Point to the parts of the body as they are mentioned and/or mime the actions.

Eight big fingers standing up tall
Two little ears to hear Mummy call
One little nose that I can blow
Ten little toes all in a row
Two short thumbs that wriggle up and
    down
Two little feet to stand on the ground
Hands to clap and eyes to see
Oh, what fun to be just me!

Follow-up

Ask the children to look carefully at a tissue, feel it and take it apart. Why do we use tissues for blowing our noses? Why don't we use drawing paper? Ask the children to find out what happens when you let a drop or two of paint fall on to the tissue.

Make a positive progress chart to show all the children who are learning or have learned to use a tissue when they blow their noses.

Washing day

Objective

To encourage familiarity with jobs done at home.

What you need

No special equipment.

What to do

Sing the following rhyme to the tune of 'Here we go round the mulberry bush'.

I went to visit some friends one day,
They only lived across the way,
They said they couldn't come out to
    play
Because it was their washing day.

This is the way they wash all day,
Wash all day, wash all day,
This is the way they wash all day,
Because it is their washing day.

Add some more verses, replacing washing with ironing, cooking, cleaning, digging, planting, shopping or any other job suggested by the children.

Follow-up

• Ask the children to think about the jobs that need doing each day in the classroom, such as clearing the tables and tidying the book-corner. What would the children feel like if they came into a dirty, untidy classroom in the morning?
• If the caretaker or cleaner is willing, invite him or her into the classroom to talk and answer questions about what needs doing around the school and how it is done. Is there any way the children could make it easier for the cleaning staff to do their job?
• The children could make 'thank you' cards for their parents or for the cleaners who keep things clean and tidy.
• Use a big empty grocery box to make a 'washing-machine' for the home corner. What kind of door will it have?

I don't want to!

Objective

To reinforce children's feelings of self.

What you need

No special equipment.

What to do

Think of a list of jobs that need doing in the house or classroom. Suggest the jobs to the children, and tell them that they can reject every job but 'feed the cat'. For example:

'Sweep the floor!'
'I don't want to!' (Unison)
'Wash the dishes!'
'I don't want to!'
'Do the shopping!'
'I don't want to!'
'Tidy the toys!'
'I don't want to!'
'Feed the cat!'
'Yes, I will.'

'Clean the windows!'
'I don't want to!'
'Make the beds!'
'I don't want to!'
'Bath the baby!'
'I don't want to!'
'Feed the cat!'
'Yes, I will.'

Repeat this format, mixing up the jobs and adding others each time, but always finishing with 'feed the cat'.

The idea of this game is that it is basically all right *not* to want to do some jobs sometimes — adults feel the same way too. But we all have to accept some jobs whatever we feel like.

Follow-up

• Talk about the jobs the children do at home and at school, and whether they like or dislike them. What would happen if no one wanted to do the dishes, sweep the floor or feed the cat?
• Read *I'm Not Going to Get Up Today* by Dr Seuss (Collins).
• Play the game again, using different kinds of food instead of jobs, with say, bread or pizza as the food children *must* eat, although they can refuse others such as rice, meat, peas or cabbage.

Going to the market

Objective

To encourage skills in remembering, sequencing and classification.

What you need

A basket, five or six foods, food cartons or pictures of foods (optional).

What to do

> I'm going to the market
> For an apple to chew,
> Is there something
> I can bring for you?

Sit with the children in a circle, and choose one child to carry the basket. Everyone says the rhyme, while the child with the basket goes around the circle, stopping at the end of each verse and asking the child he stops by for a suggestion. The foodstuffs or pictures can be helpful reminders to the children.
    The first child might suggest a . . . cake. The child with the basket sets off again, and everyone says the second verse.

> I'm going to the market
> For a cake, and an apple to chew,
> Is there something
> I can bring for you?

The next child might suggest . . . some bread.

> I'm going to the market
> For some bread, a cake, and an apple
>   to chew,
> Is there something
> I can bring for you?

Follow-up

- Collect cartons and food containers for a classroom shop, making sure they are clean and safe. Supply the shop and the home corner with notepads and pencils for writing shopping lists and bills.
- Use big boxes to make supermarket trolleys, and fit them out with wheels and axles from a construction kit.
- Read *Don't Forget the Bacon* by Pat Hutchins (Puffin).

Who uses this?

Objective

To help the children identify tools, jobs and workers.

What you need

A variety of play tools and/or real ones, such as a hammer, a spanner, scissors, a tape measure, a torch, a dentist's mirror, a thermometer or temperature strip, cotton wool, a brush, a bucket, a spirit level, a pen, a briefcase and so on.

What to do

Select six or seven tools to use at any one time. Show the children one tool and ask them what it is, who might use it, and what this person might do with it. Are there any other things the tool is used for? Do any members of the children's families use it?
    Together with the children, mime some of the actions that go with a particular tool. Play a guessing game, letting individual children mime one of the jobs for the others to guess the tool they are using.

Follow-up

● Play the game again with a variety of different hats, such as a police helmet, a traffic warden's hat, a hard hat and a nurse's hat. If necessary, explain briefly to the children what each represents.
● If insufficient objects are available, play the guessing game with posters of people at work, covering up the picture and leaving the head only exposed.

The wheels on the bus

Objective

To enjoy representing different people's behaviour.

What you need

No special equipment.

What to do

Sit the children on the floor in pairs either side of a 'gangway'. If there is space, the children could sit on chairs to sing the following song together. The odd one out is the driver.

The wheels on the bus go round and
    round,
Round and round,
Round and round,
The wheels on the bus go round and
    round,
All day long.

The horn on the bus goes honk! honk!
    honk! . . .

The mums on the bus go chatter,
    chatter, chatter . . .

The dads on the bus go nod, nod,
    nod . . .

The kids on the bus go fidget, fidget,
    fidget . . .

The wheels on the bus go round and
    round . . .

Show the children how to do the appropriate actions for the song, rotating their hands around each other for the wheels, squeezing their hands together for the horn, and pretending to be the different people in each verse.

Follow-up

● Take the children for a ride on a real bus. How much is the fare? Why do they think it is more expensive for you than for them?
● Do paintings of the local buses, and make large box models of them. Cut out a flap at the back for the engine.
● Leave out some plastic tools for mending the pretend wheels or engine, or for cleaning the buses.

Godfrey Gordon Gustavus Gore

Objective

To remind children about their responsibilities!

What you need

No special equipment.

What to do

Say the following rhyme, and encourage the children to join in with Godfrey Gordon's name and the repeated refrain of 'shut the door!'

Godfrey Gordon Gustavus Gore
(I expect you've heard that name
   before)
Was a boy who never would shut the
   door!

The wind might whistle, the wind might
   roar
And teeth be aching and throats be
   sore
But still he never would shut the door.

His father would beg, his mother
   implore,
'Godfrey Gordon Gustavus Gore
We really wish you would shut the
   door!'

They shook their heads, their hair they
   tore,
But Godfrey Gordon Gustavus Gore
Was as deaf as the lighthouse beside
   the shore.

When he walked out the folks would
   roar,
'Godfrey Gordon Gustavus Gore
Why will you never shut the door?'

They got him a boat with a sail and an
   oar
And threatened to pack off Gustavus
   Gore
To a far away place called Singapore.

But he begged for mercy, and said 'No
   more!
Please do not send me to Singapore,
I'll try to remember to shut the door'.

You can devise some appropriate actions to go with the rhyme, such as shivering in verse two, putting your hands together imploringly in verse three, shaking your head and pretending to tear your hair in verse four, and so on.

Follow-up

Do the children remember what their parents or other grown-ups tell them to do? Are some things easy to forget? Which are the things that they should *never* forget? Talk about the importance of road safety, never going home with strangers and so on.

The postman

Objective

To encourage recognition of visitors to our homes and an awareness of when they might arrive.

What you need

Old letters, postmen's caps, a big bag or sack, plastic or wooden tools, hats, a doctor's bag.

What to do

Choose a boy or girl to be the postman or postwoman. The other children can stand in a circle and recite or sing the following rhyme to the tune of 'Here we go round the mulberry bush'.

When it's morning the postman comes,
The postman comes, the postman
    comes,
When it's morning the postman comes
And leaves us all some letters.

While everyone is singing, the 'postman' goes round the circle giving out pretend or real letters.

Ask the children who else comes to our houses. Do the children know when they visit and what they do? Make up some other verses for the song, based on their suggestions, such as 'When it's Thursday, the dustmen come . . . And take the bins away', or 'When it's Christmas Santa comes . . . And leaves us all some presents', or 'When I'm sick, the doctor comes . . . And makes me soon feel better.'

Follow-up

Encourage the children to play house-visiting games in the home corner. Put out appropriate clothes and tools for postmen, doctors, service engineers and so on.

Motor skills

Chapter two

What can our bodies do? Young children are emerging from a state where motor control is not complete in either gross motor skills or precise ones. With practice, children will develop physical co-ordination.

Bending fingers, folding arms, hopping and skipping are all new skills for young children. Like all new abilities, they begin imprecisely and need practice if they are to become second nature. These activities represent both a challenge and a delight for small children. It can be very reassuring to be with others who make mistakes, fall down and get confused too; and what a lovely opportunity to *let off steam*!

Two fat gentlemen

Objective

To encourage finger play and co-ordination.

What you need

No special equipment.

What to do

Say the following rhyme with the children, doing the finger actions.

Two fat gentlemen met in the lane
[thumbs facing each other]
Bowed most politely,
[thumbs bend]
Bowed once again.
[thumbs bend]
'How do you do,
[left thumb bends]
How do you do,
[right thumb bends]
How do you do again?'
[thumbs bend]

Repeat this verse, replacing the fat gentlemen with two thin ladies (the forefingers), then two tall policemen (the middle fingers), two little children (the fourth fingers), and finally two little babies (the little fingers).

Follow-up

• Talk with the children about different customs of greeting. For example, grown-ups sometimes shake hands; families may exchange kisses or hugs; and in some Middle or Far-Eastern countries bowing is traditional. What do their parents and grandparents do when they meet the children?
• Spend a week greeting each other in the morning and saying goodbye in the afternoon by bowing to each other.

Wind the bobbin up

Objective

A simple game for the very young.

What you need

No special equipment.

What to do

Say the following rhyme with the children. The actions are fairly self-explanatory!

Wind the bobbin up
Wind the bobbin up
   [revolve hands one around the other]
Pull! Pull!
   [pull hands apart]
Clap, clap, clap.
Point to the ceiling
Point to the floor
Point to the window
Point to the door
Clap your hands together 1, 2, 3,
Put your hands upon your knee.

Follow this with some more simple games, perhaps those on pages 13 and 20.

Open them, shut them

Objective

To provide a useful starting or ending game, especially for the youngest children.

What you need

No special equipment.

What to do

Play this game sitting down. Encourage the children to use their hands to do the actions suggested by the words. In verse two they can walk their fingers up their arms, and then raise their hands as high as they can. In verse three they should let their hands float slowly down before raising them up again quickly.

Open them, shut them,
Open them, shut them,
Give a little clap.
Open them, shut them,
Open them, shut them,
Put them on your lap.

Creeping, creeping, creeping
Up to shoulders high,
Now they're going higher,
They're going to reach the sky.

Falling, falling, falling
Right down on to the ground,
Quickly pick them up again
And roll them round and round.

Follow-up

Play a guessing game with counters. Conceal one, two or three counters in your hand for the children to guess how many there are. Then open your hand to reveal them.

Tall shops

Objective

To have fun with finger play.

What you need

No special equipment.

What to do

Tall shops in the town
  [hold arms up]
Lifts moving up and down
  [one hand goes up and down]
Doors swinging round about
  [arms opening and shutting]
People moving in and out.
  [fingers walking forwards and backwards]

Follow-up

● Have the children been in a lift or on an escalator? What did it feel like?
● Make a shoebox lift for the class teddy or a doll, by attaching string to the box and either drawing it across a table top or using it with a pulley.

Punchinello

Objective

To encourage children to think of actions for themselves.

What you need

No special equipment.

What to do

The music for this song is on page 92. Stand or sit in a ring, and choose one confident child to go into the centre and perform an action. With the child in the middle, everyone sings:

What can you do, Punchinello, little
  fellow?
What can you do, Punchinello, little
  man?

The child at the centre then does an action; perhaps she claps her hands, taps her shoulders, stamps her feet or touches her knees. Some children may need ideas to start them off. Then everyone sings:

We'll do it too, Punchinello, little fellow,
We'll do it too, Punchinello, little man.

Everyone copies the action, and then either you or the original child can choose a new child to go in the centre.

Follow-up

Spend some time discussing with the children the kinds of actions our bodies can do, and demonstrate some of them. What can they do on the PE or playground equipment?

The rabbit

Objective

To encourage dexterity in finger play.

What you need

No special equipment.

What to do

Show the children how to do the actions for the following rhyme.

A little rabbit on a hill
Was bobbing up and down.
  [hand moving up and down]
His little tail was soft and white,
  [fist clenched]
His two long ears were brown,
  [two fingers waggling]
But when he heard a tiny noise
  [point to ears]
His eyes were black as coal,
  [point to eyes]
His little whiskers trembled
  [fingers waving]
And he scuttled down a hole.
  [hand behind back]

Follow-up

● Read *The Tale of the Flopsy Bunnies* by Beatrix Potter (Warne).
● Have any of the children seen Bugs Bunny on the television? What kind of rabbit is he?
● If there is a pet rabbit in school, go and have a look at his eyes, his ears and his fur. Encourage the children to make paintings and collages with fake fur fabric.

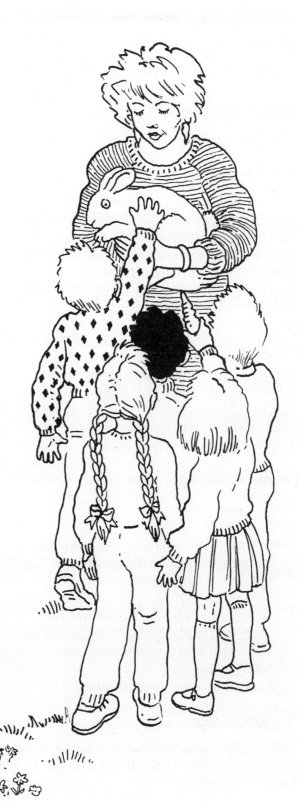

One finger, one thumb

Objective

To encourage co-ordination.

What you need

No special equipment.

What to do

This is a very energetic game, and so is best played just before playtime, or when the children need something active to do just before or after sitting still for a long time. Use it on a rainy day when everyone has been stuck in the classroom at playtime!

One finger, one thumb, keep moving,
One finger, one thumb, keep moving,
One finger, one thumb, keep moving,
We'll all be merry and bright.

One finger, one thumb, one arm, one
    leg, keep moving . . .

One finger, one thumb, one arm, one
    leg, one shake of the head, keep
    moving . . .

One finger, one thumb, one arm, one
    leg, one shake of the head, stand up,
    sit down, keep moving . . .

One finger, one thumb, one arm, one
    leg, one shake of the head, stand up,
    sit down and turn around, keep
    moving . . .
We'll all be merry and bright!

Follow-up

Follow this game with more action games if necessary, until *some* of the children's energy is used up!

This way and that way

Objective

To develop co-ordination.

What you need

No special equipment.

What to do

The music for this song is on page 92. Either you or a chosen child can initiate a movement during the verse, and the others should then copy it during the chorus. For example, you might shake both hands to the left and then to the right, clap or click your fingers.

Did you ever see a lassie (laddie)
Go this way and that way,
Did you ever see a lassie
Go this way and that?

Go this way and that way,
Go this way and that way,
Did you ever see a lassie
Go this way and that.

Follow-up

• Do some more moving in PE or movement lessons where there is more space for whole body movements. Ask the children to play the game above with a partner, copying their movements.
• Get out some mirrors, including a full-length mirror if possible. Invite the children to watch what their mirror-image does when they touch their nose, smile, frown or open their mouth. Can they draw themselves from looking in the mirror?

Shake the bed

Objective

To improve co-ordination skills and encourage co-operation with others.

What you need

No special equipment.

What to do

Shake the bed,
Shake the bed,
And turn the blanket
OVER!

Ask the children to work in pairs, holding hands with arms outstretched. For the first two lines they should shake their arms gently up and down, and then, still holding hands, they should turn so they are back to back. Then you can repeat the verse so that the children turn again to face each other. Please note that some young children's arms are very short, and they will need to be told to let go of one hand or both for the turning.

Follow-up

• Make up some bedding in the home corner and put two children in charge of the bed-making each day. Have an 'inspection' before afternoon storytime. Do the children make their beds at home?
• Encourage the children to design and make beds and bunks from cereal packets, to fit small toys and dolls. Will the beds have legs? How can the top bunk be raised above the bottom one?
• Make sets to show who sleeps in which kind of bed.

Hippity hop

Objective

To practise or learn to hop.

What you need

No special equipment.

What to do

If necessary, show the children how to hop on each foot. Hopping on alternate feet leads to skipping. Remind them about safety and the need to allow each other plenty of space. Then say the following rhyme together, hopping about as you say it.

> Hippity hop to the grocer's shop
>   *[hop]*
> To buy a jar of honey
> You can skip if you like,
>   *[give time to skip]*
> Or go on your bike,
>   *[give time to mime this]*
> But don't forget your money!
>   *[show empty hands]*

Follow-up

Read 'Hoppity' and other poems from *When We Were Very Young* by A. A. Milne (Methuen).

The ring

Objective

To give practice in co-ordinated movements.

What you need

No special equipment.

What to do

> We'll make a ring
> And all hold hands
> And show what we can do.
> We'll jump and clap
> And jump again
> Can you and you and you?
>
> The first must jump
> The second clap
> The third must jump again,
> And jump and clap
> And jump and clap
> And jump and clap again.

The children all join hands and walk around in a ring. Then they drop hands and all jump and clap and jump again as the first verse indicates.

Start the second verse by naming a child. The named child jumps as you say 'the first must jump', and then the next child claps, then the next one jumps. The next child after that also jumps, but the next one claps, and so on, following the instructions, to the end of the verse.

Repeat the rhyme, the first child this time being the one where the action left off last time. Be prepared for jumping and clapping out of order — but treat it as an occasion for fun rather than making children feel they are 'getting things wrong'.

Follow-up

Practise different types of movement in PE lessons – jumping, skipping and so on. Choose children to demonstrate their skills to the rest of the class.

Simon says

Objective

To help children to identify parts of the body.

What you need

No special equipment.

What to do

The children can stand or sit while the teacher or one child gives instructions, which are only obeyed if 'Simon says'.
- Simon says – touch your nose;
- Simon says – pat your head;
- Simon says – touch your elbow;
- Simon says – point to your eyes;
- Touch your knees!
    Some children will be caught out, and can simply be named before repeating the game, all joining in again. Try speeding up the instructions!

Follow-up

- Draw round a boy and a girl in the class, and let the children paint the outlines and put labels on the different parts of the bodies.
- Use movement lessons to see what the knees and elbows are for. What would it be like if we couldn't bend our arms and legs? Ask the children to try doing movements without bending them.

I'm a little teapot

Objective

To have fun with movement.

What you need

No special equipment.

What to do

Show the children how to do the movements that go with the following well-known rhyme.

> I'm a little teapot
> Short and stout,
> Here's my handle,
>   *[hand on hip]*
> Here's my spout.
>   *[other arm extended]*
> When I hear the tea cup
> Hear me shout,
> Lift me up
>   *[jump]*
> And pour me out!
>   *[tip to the side]*

Follow-up

Display a collection of teapots. Do the children know what they are made of? Demonstrate how they can be used to pour cold water into a cup, and let the children listen to the sound the water makes. Put a non-breakable teapot into the water tank and/or the home corner, along with some plastic cups. Let the children practise pouring. If the teapot is full, how many children could have a cup of tea?

Teddy bear, teddy bear

Objective

To give practice in sequencing actions.

What you need

No special equipment.

What to do

Say the following rhyme together, encouraging the children to do the relevant actions.

Teddy bear, teddy bear,
Touch the ground,
Teddy bear, teddy bear,
Turn around.

Teddy bear, teddy bear,
Go upstairs,
Teddy bear, teddy bear,
Say your prayers.

Teddy bear, teddy bear,
Switch out the light,
Teddy bear, teddy bear,
Say 'Goodnight'.

Traditionally this was used by older chidren as a skipping rhyme. This can be done with younger children if two adults hold the ends of the rope, or if one end of the rope is tied to a post.

Follow-up

● Make a model bed for a teddy bear with a cereal packet, and put it in a grocery box 'bedroom'. If possible, use a simple electricity kit to put a light bulb and switch in the bedroom. The children can then do the action poem with the teddy bear.
● Read *Paddington Bear* by Michael Bond (Piccolo).
● Talk with the children about their bedtime patterns (and about their fears). Do they turn out the light, or do they prefer to leave a little light on? How do they manage to make just a little bit of light?

The dragon

Objective

To encourage co-operative movements.

What you need

A dragon's mask (optional), a large space.

What to do

This is a variation on a Chinese game. It can be played at any time, but is particularly suitable at Chinese New Year.

To start the game, choose one child as the dragon's head. She may wear the dragon mask. All say 'The dragon wants a body!' (The 'head' then chooses another child, who joins on by holding on to her waist.)

Next everyone says, 'The dragon's body is longer!' (The second child chooses someone else to join him.)

Everyone says again, 'The dragon's body is *longer*!' (That child chooses another, and so on until all the children but one are joined on.) Then everyone says, 'The dragon wants a tail!' When all the children are joined on, the 'head' leads them in a walk around the room, with the children following on.

There are two ways of finishing this game.

● With younger children, shout 'Tail!' The 'head' then breaks off from the front (giving the mask, if she is wearing one, to the next child) and joins the end to become the tail.

● With older children, again shout 'Tail!', but the children stay joined on to the 'head', if they can, while she tries to chase round and capture the unwilling 'tail'.

Follow-up

● Make Chinese dragon masks with short cylinders of card or sugar paper, giving them large eye-holes and mouths. The children can paint them brightly, and decorate them with streamers of tissue or crêpe paper.

● Make a giant dragon with grocery boxes laid in a row. Invite the children to measure it with strides and footsteps.

● Can the children suggest what they could use to make a big dragon's egg?

Auntie Monica

Objective

To enjoy the sheer pleasure of movement.

What you need

No special equipment.

What to do

Sing the following song to the tune of 'My old man's a dustman', or any tune with a similar rhythm.

> Oh, I have an Auntie,
> An Auntie Monica,
> And when she goes out shopping
> They all say
> 'Oooh, La! La!'
>
> Because her feather's swinging
> *[wave one arm backwards and forwards above the head]*
> Her feather's swinging so
> Because her feather's swinging
> Her feather's swinging so.
>
> Ooooh, I have an Auntie . . .
>
> Because her basket's swinging
> *[swing one arm as if swinging a basket]*
> Her basket's swinging so . . .
>
> Oooooooooh, I have an Auntie . . .
>
> Because her skirt is swinging
> *[swing skirt if wearing one; otherwise swing both arms]*
> Her skirt is swinging so . . .

The 'Oh' in the chorus gets longer each time, and the 'Ooh, La, La' is quite loud throughout the song. This song is fun to show off to other classes or to parents.

Follow-up

● Make a collection of feathers, especially some big ones, and encourage the children to look at them and feel them with their fingers and against their faces.
● If there are enough feathers, use them in a collage of Auntie Monica, or to decorate other paintings suggested by the children.

Social skills

Chapter three

Learning social skills helps young children to let go of their egocentric view of the universe and accept a shift of emphasis to other children and the whole group. It is important that the child learns to trust and to value others – their needs, interests, skills and difficulties. Children will discover that they can take the lead with the group or cede status to others, co-operate and show tolerance, take turns and wait. They will apply what they have learned with their peers to their dealings with other groups of people in other places.

It's me today

Objective

To encourage self-esteem and valuing others.

What you need

No special equipment.

What to do

Choose some children to praise individually. These may be:
• the weekly or daily helpers;
• a group of five to ten children (working down the register) in a session held once a week;
• the whole class, in a session held once a month.

At a convenient time, when everyone is gathered together, ask the chosen children to stand up in front of the others.

Make some positive statements about each of the children, and ask the rest of the children to clap, either for each individual, or for the whole group. Some examples of statements might be:
• 'Jane has been so smiley today, she's made me really happy';
• 'Bhavi is so good at lining up at the door – I'm very proud of him';
• 'Susie has such a good memory – she always brings her folder back for a new book'.

Follow-up

Once this ritual has been established, invite the other children to add one or two compliments too, before clapping.

Giving gifts

Objective

To provide practice in giving and receiving.

What you need

A lot of classroom or borrowed toys, tissue and/or old wrapping paper, sticky tape, sticky shapes, glitter, paint, pieces of card, string, a hole punch, name cards for each of the children.

What to do

Towards Christmas or another festival, help each child to wrap up a pretend present (one of the classroom toys). You will need plenty of time and/or classroom support for this, but it gives excellent opportunities for the children to learn about shapes and materials.

Take two name cards at random and let the two children named use the cards to copy each other's names on to a gift tag – 'To Jason, from Rachel' and 'To Rachel, from Jason'. Carry on drawing pairs of name cards until every child has written a tag. Punch a hole in each tag and thread them with string. Display the pretend presents and gift tags on a table or by the Christmas tree.

On the giving day, which might be at the end of term, ask each child to bring in two biscuits or a piece of fruit wrapped in foil and put them with their 'gift'. Then take turns to read the tags and give out the pretend presents. Before unwrapping them, can the children tell what they are from the shape or the feel of the parcels?

Let the children unwrap the parcels, replace the toys, and then eat their real fruit or biscuit gift.

Follow-up

• Ask the children what it feels like to give a friend a present. What does it feel like to be given one? Have they all said 'Thank you'?
• Read 'King John' by A. A. Milne, from *Now We Are Six* (Methuen).

I'd like to give

Objective

To provide practice in giving (at any time of the year).

What you need

A whiteboard and felt-tipped pens, or a blackboard and chalks.

What to do

Choose one child and write his name at the top of the board. Invite the other children to think of presents that he might like to receive. Encourage all the children to join in. Write down some of the suggestions, sticking to a predetermined number, such as four.

Repeat the exercise with another name. This can be done over a few days until all the children have had a turn. Then all the lists can be displayed.

Follow-up

• Each child could have a wish about what he or she would like to receive best in all the world, and this could be added to the bottom of his or her list.
• Ask the children to draw or paint some of the gifts they have been 'given' or their wished-for present.

Down by the river

Objective

To help children to get used to choosing a partner.

What you need

No special equipment.

What to do

Sit in a circle with one child at the centre pretending to 'wash clothes'. Sing the following rhyme – the music is on page 93.

Down by the river where the green
    grass grows
There sits [Sarah] washing her clothes.
She sings, she sings, she sings so sweet,
She calls to her playmate across the
    street.

[Darren, Darren,] won't you come to
    tea?
Come next Thursday at half-past three.
Ice-cream, cream cakes, anything you
    please;
Won't we have a lovely time at half-
    past three?

When called, Darren goes into the centre with Sarah. At the end of that verse Sarah returns to the ring and the game begins again with Darren alone in the middle.

Follow-up

Do some work with a large teaching clock to show the children what is meant by 'o'clock' and 'half-past'. Just use the big hand with the youngest children – symbolic time is difficult when they only have a vestigial idea about time.

Isn't it funny?

Objective

To help children learn to take turns.

What you need

A large transparent plastic jar or container labelled 'honey'.

What to do

Ask the children to sit in a circle, with one child at the centre and the honey jar placed behind her. Then they can all say the following rhyme.

Isn't it funny that a bear likes honey!
Buzz, buzz, buzz
I wonder why he does?
Go to sleep, Mr Bear!
    *[the bear shuts her eyes while you point at
    another child who silently goes and steals the
    honey]*
Wake up, Mr Bear!
Someone's stolen your honey!

The bear chases the 'thief' around the outside of the circle back to his place. The original bear sits in the thief's place; the thief becomes the bear.

Follow-up

● Bring in some honey for the children to smell and taste.
● What colour is honey? What colour paint do the children think would be the nearest? Can they mix some paint to make the right colour? They can use this paint to make pictures of honey jars.
● Read the children a story about Winnie the Pooh and his honeypots (from *Winnie the Pooh* by A. A. Milne, Methuen).

Who's missing?

Objective

To encourage identification with the group and other children within the group.

What you need

Two large objects for the children to hide behind, such as a bookcase and a screen.

What to do

Choose two 'detectives' to go out of sight of the whole group. Ask another child to hide without being seen by the detectives, who then come back and guess who is missing.

This is a particularly good game to play when the group is fairly (not totally) new to each other; or when they go into a new situation, such as a new class or a new room. It will reinforce the identity of the group.

Follow-up

● Play 'What's missing?' with objects on a tray (see page 66).
● Play 'Spot the mistake' (see page 44).

Where am I?

Objective

To help build trust and develop orientation.

What you need

A soft scarf to be a blindfold.

What to do

Ask the children to sit to one side of the room. Blindfold one child and turn him around three times.

Two other children can then take him by the hands and take him for a little roundabout walk to a spot such as the book corner or the window, where they stop. Can the blindfolded child guess where he is?

Repeat this with other children taking it in turns to be blindfolded.

Follow-up

● What does it feel like when you can't see? How did the guide-children keep the blindfolded ones safe?
● Ask a sight-disabled person to come and visit with his or her dog, and show how the dog behaves like the person's eyes.
● Write to the Royal National Institute for the Blind for further information and ideas for caring for their members.

Elephants on a string

Objective

To give children practice in choosing and co-operating.

What you need

No special equipment.

What to do

Ask the children to hold hands and move round in a ring. Choose one child to stand in the centre and sing the following song together (the music is on page 94).

One elephant went out to play
Upon a piece of string one day.
She thought it such tremendous fun
She called for another elephant to
    come.

The first child then chooses a second, and they hold hands and dance round in the centre. Everyone sings the rhyme again — 'Two elephants went out to play . . .'. Then the second child chooses a third, and so on through more verses of the song, until you have ten elephants (or another convenient number). Then you can sing:

Ten elephants went out to play
Upon a piece of string one day.
But suddenly . . .
THE STRING BROKE!

All the elephants tumble down and then go back to their places in the big circle.

Follow-up

● Bring in a variety of types of string to look at. Would any of them support even *one* elephant? Why not?
● Unravel the strings and let the children look at them closely. They can cut the threads into different lengths and use them to make stick-on pictures and shapes.
● Stick some pieces of string very firmly on to small blocks of wood, and let the children use them for printing.
● Read *Elmer: The Story of a Patchwork Elephant* by David McKee (Andersen Press).

Mary's alone in the ring

Objective

To give experience of choosing.

What you need

No special equipment.

What to do

Ask the children to join hands in a ring, and choose one child to stand in the centre. All the other children should then walk round her, singing:

Mary's alone in the ring,
Mary's alone in the ring.
Who'll go and play with her?
Who'll go and stay with her?
Mary's alone in the ring.

Mary then chooses Jack, who goes and joins her in the centre. The two join hands and skip round in the middle, while everyone sings:

Jack will join Mary and play,
Jack will join Mary today.
Jack will play with her,
Jack will stay with her,
Jack will join Mary and play.

Then Mary goes back to join the circle of children, and the game continues:

Jack is alone in the ring
Jack is alone in the ring . . .

Follow-up

Start a discussion about dealing with playtime friendship needs by offering one of your own experiences, and inviting the children's comments. You might say, 'I remember once when nobody wanted to play with me in the playground . . .', 'I saw Bansuk being really nice to Charlie in the playground yesterday', or 'Sometimes I like to play by myself . . .'.

The farmer's in his den

Objective

To encourage choosing and co-operating.

What you need

No special equipment.

What to do

Ask the children to stand in a ring, with one child in the middle as the farmer. The other children should hold hands and walk around him as they sing. At the end of each verse another child is chosen to join the others in the centre and hold hands with them. The last verse is sung while everyone who can reach *gently* pats the 'cheese-child', who then becomes the farmer for the next game.

The farmer's in his den
The farmer's in his den
Ee-o, Ee-enjio,
The farmer's in his den.

The farmer wants a wife . . .
The wife wants a child . . .
The child wants a nurse . . .
The nurse wants a dog . . .
The dog wants a cat . . .
The cat wants a mouse . . .
The mouse wants some cheese . . .
. . . We all pat the cheese.

Although this game looks as though it supports stereotypical gender roles, in reality either a boy or a girl can act any of the parts, whether farmer or nurse. You may prefer to substitute 'husband' for 'wife'.

Follow-up

● Help the children to make a model farm with a card base, packets and boxes for farm buildings and clay or Plasticine animals.
● Plan a visit to a farm.
● Sing 'Old Macdonald had a farm'.

The huntsman

Objective

Awareness of different human attitudes.

What you need

No special equipment.

What to do

Sing the following rhyme with the children, doing the actions.

In a cottage in a wood
   [make roof shape with hands]
A little old man at the window stood
   [form a window with thumbs and forefingers]
Saw a rabbit running by
   [shade eyes with hand]
Knocking at his door.
   [knock with fist]

'Help me! Help me! Help me!' he said,
   [arms stretched out]
'Before the huntsman shoots me dead!'
   [pretend to shoot]
BANG!
'Come little rabbit, come with me,
   [beckon inwards]
Happy we shall be.'
   [clap in rhythm]

Follow-up

● Why do the children think the huntsman might want to kill the rabbit? What if the huntsman were a farmer and the rabbits were eating all his lettuces?
● Read *The Tale of the Flopsy Bunnies* by Beatrix Potter (Warne).
● Divide the children into groups, each of which is a pride of lions. Let them decide who will be the lions, lionesses and cubs. Then you can stalk them, pretending to be a hunter. They can behave in any way they feel is appropriate — growl, roar, look after their cubs, and so on. Then ask them what the lions felt like being hunted. What would they like to say to a real hunter?
● Find information books about lions and other animals.

Let's build

Objective

To develop co-operation and the ability to work as a group.

What you need

A large space to work in.

What to do

This activity is particularly suitable for children at the older end of the age range. Ask the children to form groups of three or four. Give each group the name of a structure, and encourage the children to help each other to make that object, using only their bodies. For example, you might ask them to make an aeroplane, a bridge, a house, a car, a tree, a chair or a crane.

Some of the structures will need discussion. Ask the children in each group what their object looks like, what it is for and how it works, and then they can try to make it. Go round to each group and praise the way the children support each other.

Give each group a chance to show the whole class one of the structures they have built.

Follow-up

In the same groups, the children can use everyday materials to make a model of one of the structures. Then they can paint and display it.

Little bird

Objective

To help the children to quieten down.

What you need

No special equipment.

What to do

Use this and other short poems when the children are gathered together, but not yet listening quietly. Start the poem firmly, doing the actions, and as the children join in, bring your voice down. Repeat the poem a second time very quietly.

> I saw a little bird
> Going hop, hop, hop,
> *[one hand bobbing up and down]*
> And I said, 'Little bird,
> Will you stop, stop, stop?'
> *[look enquiringly at the children]*
>
> And I said, 'Little bird,
> Will you stay, stay, stay?'
> But she shook her head
> *(children shake heads]*
> And she flew away.
> *[one hand 'flies away']*

Follow-up

If you have a winter bird table or a grassy area nearby, let the children observe the birds. How do the birds walk, fly and feed?

The waiting game: 1

Objective

To encourage self-control.

What you need

A great deal of patience!

What to do

Many teachers do this automatically without thinking of it as a game. It can be played with very young children who are new into nursery or mainstream school, or with children who arrive rumbustiously in Year 1, Year 2 or later.

Explain that when you all come together for the register, for storytime or to receive instructions, you will play 'the waiting game'. You will wait until each child decides by himself or herself to be still and quiet.

Then wait.

And wait some more.

Wait even more.

It is important that you neither answer the children nor remind them to be quiet. You might just look at the wall, or at them, but very quietly and without impatience or frustration.

Just wait.

Try not to worry about the time being spent in this way — it is immensely valuable if the children can settle down by themselves. If people come into the classroom while this is going on, ask them if possible to come back later.

It will be necessary to play this game often at first until the children begin to quieten immediately, and even then they will need reminders of the waiting game from time to time. However, the long-term benefits are *enormous*.

Follow-up

You can also play the lining-up game. In this game you ask everyone to line up at the door, walking carefully, standing still and keeping quiet.

If *anyone* spoils the game, everyone goes back to the mat or to their seats, without recrimination, and you play the game again.

Once again, if anyone does not play the game, go back to the mat, and so on . . . and so on . . . .

It is vitally important that there is no negative feedback or telling-off for anyone, simply that you will repeat the game until *everyone* can do it. *Don't* give in or give up! Achieving this not only makes life more enjoyable in the classroom, but the children themselves also experience a sense of pride in their ability to queue up quickly and quietly.

The waiting game: 2

Objective

To develop the children's self-control and help them become quiet.

What you need

No special equipment.

What to do

There are often children who cannot attain the necessary level of self-control by playing the waiting game. They may even become very disruptive. If that is the case, try adding quietening actions during the waiting period. For example:

- Everyone lie down flat.
- Close your eyes.
- Listen — listen to that car far away.
- Listen — listen to the footsteps going down the corridor.
- Listen — listen to the heater in the classroom.
- Press your hands on the floor.
- Put your hands on your legs.
- In a minute you can slowly, slowly, open your eyes . . .
- Open them now.
- In a minute you can slowly, slowly, slowly, sit up . . .
- Sit up now.
- In a minute you can slowly, slowly, slowly, slowly, stand up . . .
- Stand up now.

   With each phrase, drop your voice both in volume and pitch, and slow down until you are speaking softly, quietly and slowly. Leave longer pauses before each instruction.

Follow-up

At the end of this activity, maintain the level of quietness by continuing to use a low voice.

Language skills and understanding

Chapter four

For young children, expressing themselves and communicating meaning is an imperfect skill as yet. The child's knowledge of vocabulary and syntax is still developing, and representing objects and events in the symbolic form of words is difficult, demanding and stimulating. Games can give an opportunity to repeat and extend language functions, and can thus be a useful aid to learning. During language games children will use words to recall, express, explain, question and sequence their thoughts. Children get a chance to develop skills of pronunciation and to use language purposefully in an atmosphere of fun.

Guess the story

Objective

To encourage recall and give examples of summarising.

What you need

A list of famous fairy stories and nursery rhymes.

What to do

Ask the children to see if they can recognise which story you are talking about, if you just give a brief summary of the plot. If they are stumped, give them more details until they guess correctly. For example, you could say, 'This story is about a princess who lived in a forest with seven little men.' If they don't guess at once, say, 'She fell asleep after eating a poisoned apple . . .'.

Follow-up

• Can the children summarise stories for the others to guess?
• Display large posters illustrating well-known stories and legends without their titles for the children to identify. What clues can they see in the picture to help them to guess correctly?
• The children could paint pictures of their favourite story or rhyme for the class to identify at story time. (This needs care — don't go on guessing too long. Try saying, 'I think I know, but can you tell me to be sure?')

Spot the mistake

Objective

To develop listening skills and recall.

What you need

A collection of nursery rhymes or poems known to you and the children.

What to do

Start saying a nursery rhyme, but go wrong somewhere. Let the children call out the proper word. For example:

Sing a song of ten pence,
A pocket full of flour,
Four and twenty blue birds . . .

Hey diddle, diddle,
The cat and the guitar,
The cow climbed over the moon . . .

Ask the children what the real words mean. Do they rhyme? Say the rhyme again, emphasising the rhyming words.

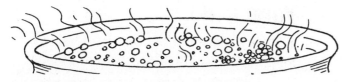

Play rhyming games with the children. Can they think of words to rhyme with cat? Ring? Hair?

NB: Children may offer words beginning with the same letter — they're getting the idea, so they deserve praise along with an explanation and another example. Some children may offer words associated with the core-word, perhaps linking 'cat' with 'dog' or 'miaow'. This also deserves praise and an explanation.

Follow-up

Write out some favourite nursery rhymes in a large book and let individual children decorate the pages with pictures or patterns.

Magic spells

Objective

To encourage children to express wishes and fantasies.

What you need

A large saucepan or garden pot, a few objects, including perhaps a cushion, a curtain ring, a small box and a large polythene bag (with holes for safety), a large wooden spoon.

What to do

Ask the children to form a ring, and put the magic pot in the centre. Say the magic verse, and after each repeat, the children can take it in turns to put something into the magic pot and turn it into their magic wish.

Onions, beetles, bad eggs too,
Mix them in a magic stew.
Fire and smoke all red and blue,
That will cook our magic stew.

For example, the child might say, 'I'm putting in a magic apple', and then, taking something out of the magic pot, 'This is a pussy-cat now'. The child should show the others, who clap. If the child takes out the curtain ring, he could put it on and pretend to have changed himself, saying 'Now I am a superhero', for example. If the children get stuck for an idea, make one or two suggestions.

Follow-up

Make a class book of spells decorated by the children.

We're going on a bear hunt

Objective

To give children experience of action verbs, sounds and prepositions.

What you need

No special equipment.

What to do

Ask the children to sit down and help you provide the sound effects for this poem.

> We're going on a bear hunt
> Tap, tap, tap, tap
> *[tapping on the knees]*
> We're going on a bear hunt
> And I'm not scared.
>
> We're going down the garden path
> Stamp, stamp, stamp, stamp
> *[tapping with feet on the floor]*
> We're going down the garden path
> And I'm not scared.
>
> We're going across the wooden bridge
> Clop, clop, clop, clop
> *[tapping on the thighs]*
> We're going across the wooden bridge
> And I'm not scared.
>
> We're going through the long grass
> Swish, swish, swish, swish
> *[loud swishing sounds]*
> We're going through the long grass
> And I'm not scared.
>
> We're going through the squelchy mud
> Slurp, slurp, slurp, slurp . . .
> *[sucking sounds]*
>
> We're swimming through the deep, deep lake
> Swim, swim, swim, swim . . .
> *[arm movements to represent swimming]*
>
> We're creeping through the dark, dark forest
> Creep, creep, creep, creep
> *[whisper]*
> We're creeping through the dark, dark forest . . .
> OH! THERE'S A BEAR! (Scream!)

(The poem is now reversed but using only the first two lines of each verse, with speech and actions done very fast.)

> We're swimming through the deep,
>   deep lake,
> Swim, swim, swim, swim
> We're going through the squelchy
>   mud,
> Slurp, slurp, slurp, slurp

(and so on, until . . .)

> We're going up the garden path
> And SLAM THE DOOR!

Follow-up

• Look at some percussion instruments with the children and let them suggest appropriate ones to represent the various sounds.
• Read *We're Going On A Bear Hunt* by Michael Rosen and Helen Oxenbury (Walker Books).
• Make 'feely' books to illustrate the story, using appropriate materials for each verse, such as pieces of sponge for the mud, lolly sticks for the bridge, and so on.

If I were . . .

Objective

To develop children's skill in using 'if' constructions, and their skills of classification.

What you need

No special equipment.

What to do

Choose a category, such as animals, plants and flowers, or toys.

Begin by saying, for example, 'If I were a flower, I would be a daffodil'. Then ask the children to contribute by saying which sort of flower or plant they would like to be. Later, if appropriate, the children could be invited to say why, but it can hold up the game if this is included earlier.

Follow-up

• Make a collection of objects which come into your chosen category, such as flowers and plants.
• Do sorting activities using simple criteria such as red/not red. Older children could use a sorting program on the computer.
• Read *If I Were a Penguin* by Heidi Goennel (Little, Brown), and *Sometimes I wish* by J. Moore (Deutsch).

Arabella Miller

Objective

To encourage pronunciation skills and rhyming in an enjoyable context.

What you need

No special equipment.

What to do

Say the following rhyme with the children, and encourage them to join in with the actions suggested below.

> Little Arabella Miller
> Found a little caterpillar.
> *[forefinger of one hand creeps over the back of the other hand]*
> 'Oh,' said Arabella Miller,
> 'What a pretty caterpillar!'
>
> Little Arabella Miller
> Found a little golden slipper.
> *[pretend to pick up slipper and look at it]*
> 'Oh', said Arabella Miller,
> 'What a pretty little slipper.'
>
> Little Arabella Miller
> Met a great big HUGE gorilla.
> *[arms stretched out wide]*
> 'OH!' said Arabella Miller,
> 'What a GIANT big gorilla!'

There is an alternative version of 'Arabella Miller' with only one verse, which goes as follows:

> Little Arabella Miller
> Found a hairy caterpillar.
> First it crawled upon her mother,
> Then upon her baby brother.
> 'Oh,' said Arabella Miller,
> 'What a hairy caterpillar!'

Follow-up

Introduce the children to some tongue twisters, such as the following.
- Red lorry, yellow lorry.
- Red leather, yellow leather.
- Silky socks and shiny shoes.
- She sells sea shells on the sea shore.
- Peter Piper picked a peck of pickled peppers.
- Round and round the rugged rock the ragged rascal ran.

Say the tongue twisters through slowly at first, gradually speeding up if the children are able.

Where's my hand?

Objective

To give the children practice in using prepositions.

What you need

No special equipment.

What to do

Play this game first with all the children following the instructions together. For example, say:
- Put your hand . . . in your pocket.
- Put your hand . . . on your head.
- Take your hand . . . off your head.
- Put your hand . . . in front of your face.
- Put your hand . . . under your jumper.
- Put your hand . . . behind your back.
- Put your hand . . . over your shoulder.
- Put your hand . . . between your knees.

With younger children use a few prepositions at a time, such as on, behind and under. Then ask individual children to take turns to put their hand somewhere, while the others describe where they have put it. For example, 'Under your foot', 'Under your shoe', 'Behind your head' or 'In front of your chest.'

'Through' can be tricky without using something like a hoop, or saying 'through the air'.

Follow-up

Reinforce the use and understanding of prepositions when lining up at the door. For example, you could say: 'Jack, go in front of Daniel; Meg, go beside Lisa; Jo, go behind Frank.'

- Make a display with everyday materials such as boxes, packets and tubes. Each day before school starts put a colourful building block in a different place in the display, and ask the children to describe where it is in relation to the other parts of the display.
- Let the children play this game together, with one child closing her eyes and the other placing the block somewhere in the display.

In and out the dusty bluebells

Objective

To reinforce the concept of 'in and out'.

What you need

No special equipment.

What to do

Sing the following rhyme with the children. The music is on page 94.

In and out the dusty bluebells
In and out the dusty bluebells
In and out the dusty bluebells
I will be your master.

Tippy tippy tap tap on your shoulder
Tippy tippy tap tap on your shoulder
Tippy tippy tap tap on your shoulder
I will be your master.

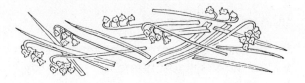

The children should stand in a ring with their arms raised, holding hands to make arches. One child starts off, weaving in and out of the ring under the arches, while everyone sings the song. When they get to 'I will be your master', the child stands behind the nearest person. Then he taps her on the shoulder in time to the words of the second verse. The second child joins on to the first one and follows in and out of the arches. At the end of the next verse both children tap others on the shoulder, and the game goes on until the ring is empty. Alternatively, you may wish to restart the game after the third or fourth verse.

Follow-up

• With older children, look at information books showing bridges and buildings with arches. Can the children find arches anywhere in or around the school?
• Encourage the children to use the edges of margarine tubs and other containers for printing with paint. Cut some of the tubs to give arch shapes as well as circles.

This is a hat

Objective

To encourage skill in responding quickly and anticipating.

What you need

Props such as a hat, or another object with a monosyllabic name, such as a toy, pen or book.

What to do

Sit with the children in a ring and pass the object around, repeating this dialogue each time the object is passed on.
First child: This is a hat.
Second child: A what?
First child: A hat.

The second child then takes the hat and offers it to the third child, saying, 'This is a hat.' The dialogue then continues around the ring.

Follow-up

Reinforce the children's response to this game at story time by showing some more unusual objects and saying, for example, 'This is a drum', 'A what?' and so on.

Guess, guess!

Objective

To develop children's use and understanding of adjectives.

What you need

Familiar objects, a large drawstring shoe-bag or shopping bag.

What to do

Show the objects to the children before they go into the bag. Discuss them, and together choose adjectives for each of them. For example, a teddy could be 'big and soft', a pencil 'long and thin', and a pine cone 'prickly and small'.

Say the following rhyme together and ask individual children to find the object described. For example, you might say:

Guess, guess!
What's inside?
Big and soft
Trying to hide.

The child then fishes in the bag to find the teddy, and holds it until a new game begins. You can then ask another child to find 'long and thin', and so on.

Limit the variables, keeping the objects familiar at first, and then introducing new ones a few at a time. Show the children the objects to begin with, and then introduce some unseen ones for the children to identify by their descriptions alone.

Follow-up

• Emphasise describing words in stories or in the comments you or the children write under their paintings or models; for example, 'Jamie painted a red flower', or 'Anne made a tall model'.
• Do sorting activities, using categories such as big/little, big/round, or for older children, big/round/soft.

And all because . . .

Objective

To encourage understanding of sequences and consequences.

What you need

Claves or similar percussion instruments.

What to do

Ask the children to sit in a circle, leaving a little space round the outside. Two children can be chosen to sit at the centre.

All the children mime the sequence described in the rhyme below. Some of them could act as a clock, making 'tick-tock' noises or beating the time using claves. In the last verse, the two children sitting in the centre come out of the circle and go round the outside until they reach their own places and sit down. This isn't a race – so speak more slowly if the children need more time to get round.

I had a bad dream
So I woke up late.

I woke up late
So I got up late.

I got up late
So I got washed late.

I got washed late
So my breakfast was late.

My breakfast was late
So I came out late.

I came out late
So I was late for school.

DONG! DONG!
DONG! DONG!
And all because of my BIG, BAD
 DREAM!

Follow-up

- Try making up alternative sequenced events appropriate to the children. For example:

I was good at my Nan's
So she gave me some sweets.

I was good in the car
So they gave me some sweets.

. . . Then I ate all the sweets
And I felt really BAD!

And all because I was good at my
    Nan's.

In this case children could role-play members of the family.
- Encourage the children to paint a sequence of pictures to tell a story.

Mr Lynn is very thin

Objective

To increase children's familiarity with adjectives.

What you need

No special equipment.

What to do

Say the following rhyme together. The children can use their hands or their whole bodies to act out the parts of the different men.

Mr Lynn is very thin,
Mr Pratt is very fat,
Mr Cort is very short,
Mr Hall is very tall,
Mr Dent is very bent,
Mr Waite is very straight.

Follow-up

Draw large figures of Mr Lynn and friends on sugar paper for the children to paint. Then you can pin them up with the appropriate label: 'Mr Pratt is very fat', and so on.

Mr. Waite   Mr. Lynn   Mr. Hall   Mr. Dent   Mr. Cort   Mr. Pratt

Mathematical skills and understanding

Chapter five

Mathematics in the form of size, shape and number is a dominant dimension of our lives. Acquiring mathematical knowledge helps us gain control over our world, and in the early years, foundations can be laid for an appreciation of the beauty of mathematics for years to come. Games give an opportunity for knowledge and skills to grow without provoking anxiety about 'getting it wrong'.

Five little soldiers

Objective

To use finger play to help with counting.

What you need

No special equipment.

What to do

Say this rhyme together, using one hand for the soldiers, and the thumb of the other for the sergeant.

> Five little soldiers
> Stand in a row,
> *[five fingers extended]*
> Three stand up straight,
> *[middle, ring and little finger stay up]*
> Two bend low.
> *[forefinger and thumb bend down]*
> Along comes the sergeant
> *[bring other thumb towards hand]*
> And what do you think?
> Up pop the soldiers
> *[forefinger and thumb upright again]*
> As quick as a wink!

Repeat the rhyme with the numbers changed; for example, 'Two stand up straight, Three bend low'.

Follow-up

● Dramatise the poem, with five children as soldiers, and one as the sergeant.

● Make a counting aid by folding some A4 sheets of paper in half lengthways, and then into five, with folds about 6cm apart. Make a person-shaped template to fit the top rectangle, and let the children draw round this if they can. Then you can help them cut it out, leaving the hands joined to make a row of five figures. Let the children colour them in with felt-tippped pens, trying to make each little paper girl or boy different. Use them for counting by holding a row up, then folding one, two or three back, and asking 'How many children now?'

Five fat sausages

Objective

To give practice in counting down from five.

What you need

No special equipment.

What to do

Sing the following rhyme with the children, to the tune of 'Ten green bottles'. Use fingers to represent the sausages.

> Five fat sausages frying in a pan,
> Five fat sausages frying in a pan,
> And if one fat sausage
> Should suddenly go 'Bang!'
> *[Loud clap]*
> There'd be four fat sausages
> Frying in a pan.
>
> Four fat sausages . . . etc.

Follow-up

• For older children, try counting down in twos from ten:

Ten fat sausages frying in the pan,
One went 'Pop!'
And another went 'Bang!'
Eight fat sausages . . .

• Cook some vegetarian and cocktail sausages, and let the children look at them before and after cooking. What changes can they see? What do the sausages smell like before cooking? After?
• Make some Plasticine sausages and burgers for the home corner, and leave two small frying pans and wooden spatulas there.
• Play 'Sausages' (see page 12).

Bobby Shaftoe

Objective

To encourage recognition and understanding of 'none', 'one' and 'two'.

What you need

A shoebox or eggbox, two Plasticine or modelling clay eggs.

What to do

Sing or recite 'Bobby Shaftoe':

Bobby Shaftoe's gone to sea,
Silver buckles on his knee,
He'll come back and marry me,
Bonny Bobby Shaftoe.

Bobby Shaftoe had a hen,
Cock-a-doodle-doodle-den,
She lays eggs for gentlemen
But NONE for Bobby Shaftoe.
[all show empty hands]

Repeat the last verse several times, deciding with the children beforehand whether Bobby Shaftoe will get one, two or no eggs. Use the shoebox or eggbox and the model eggs to remind the children of the number. Then they can complete the song, perhaps showing one finger and singing, 'And ONE for Bobby Shaftoe.'

Give the box and the eggs to different children and repeat the last verse so that they can choose the number of eggs.

Follow-up

• Make some modelling clay eggs and let the children count them into eggboxes.
• Ask the children to use white and yellow paint to paint fried eggs on blue card plates.

Five currant buns

Objective

To give children practice in counting down to zero.

What you need

No special equipment.

What to do

Ask the children to stand in a ring, and choose five 'currant buns' and a baker to stand in the middle. Then say the following rhyme together, doing the actions.

Five currant buns in the baker's shop
[all show five fingers]
Big and round with sugar on the top
[all describe a big circle with their hands and tap their heads at 'sugar']
[Jamie] came with his penny one day
[a chosen child goes up to the baker]
He bought a currant bun
[pays the baker]
And he took it right away.
[leads a 'currant bun' back to the ring]

Sing the rhyme again with four, three, two and one currant buns. The final verse goes as follows:

No currant buns in the baker's shop,
Big and round with sugar on the top,
Some children came with their pennies
  one day,
But the baker said 'There are no more
  left today.'

Follow-up

The following recipe for currant scones could be used for classroom cooking.

Use a commercially prepared shortcrust pastry mix or 125g margarine rubbed into eight tablespoons of self-raising flour. Add a pinch of salt, half a teaspoon of baking powder, two tablespoons of sultanas or currants, and enough water to make a mixture that will roll out. Cut the dough with pastry cutters and cook the scones in a moderate oven for about twelve to fifteen minutes or until cooked.

Ten in the bed

Objective

To give practice in counting down from ten.

What you need

No special equipment

What to do

Ask the children to sit in a ring, and choose ten to lie side by side close to one side of the ring. Ask one of the ten to be the 'little one'. Then everyone can sing the following rhyme.

> There were ten in the bed
> And the little one said,
> 'Roll over! Roll over!'
>
> So they all rolled over
> And one fell out . . .
> *[they all turn over and the furthest child gets up and joins the ring]*
> There were nine in the bed
> And the little one said . . .

Carry on in the same way, until:

> There was one in the bed
> And the little one said,
> 'Goodnight! Goodnight!'

Follow-up

- Get the children to do family portraits, and mount and display them along the wall.
- Older children could visit a nearby art gallery and look at the portraits there. One of the custodians might give brief histories of the people portrayed.

Get into twos

Objective

To reinforce counting skills.

What you need

No special equipment.

What to do

Ask the children to walk quietly around the available space. At the call, 'Twos!' or 'Threes!', the children have to find partners to make up the required grouping. Stress that they should choose partners from nearby.

Emphasise the number by chanting, for example, '3,3,3,3,3,3 . . . and one left with me!' Select numbers with which you know the children will probably be able to cope.

Follow-up

Read and sing about Noah's Ark and the animals going in two by two. Dramatise the story.

One potato, two potato

Objective

To encourage counting skills.

What you need

No special equipment.

What to do

Show the children how to make their hands into fists and use them to count by moving them alternately one on top of the other. Say the following rhyme together:

One potato, two potato,
Three potato, four,
Five potato, six potato,
Seven potato more.

Follow-up

• Bring in some large baking potatoes, clean them and use them for measuring and balancing.
• Ask each child to bring in a potato for baking, and observe the potatoes before and after cooking.
• Talk with the children about other occasions when we count up to seven. For example, there are seven days in a week, and seven colours in the rainbow. Seven is counted as a 'lucky' number too — can the children suggest why?

Apple, apple

Objective

To give practice in counting and estimating 'more' and 'less'.

What you need

Airflow balls or apples, a string bag or small basket.

What to do

Choose one child to be the apple tree, while the others stand in a ring around her. Give her four, five or six apples. During the rhyme the 'tree' can give or roll apples to another child of her choice. At the end of each verse, ask how many have come off the tree, and how many are left on the tree.

There are lots of lovely apples
Hanging on the tree
Along comes the wind
And blows them down for me.

Follow-up

Bring in different apples for the children to look at, feel, smell and count with. Cut some open so they can see inside, and divide some into quarters for the children to taste. Let them see what happens if pieces are exposed to the air during the day. Leave some whole and halved apples on the table for the children to draw or paint from life.

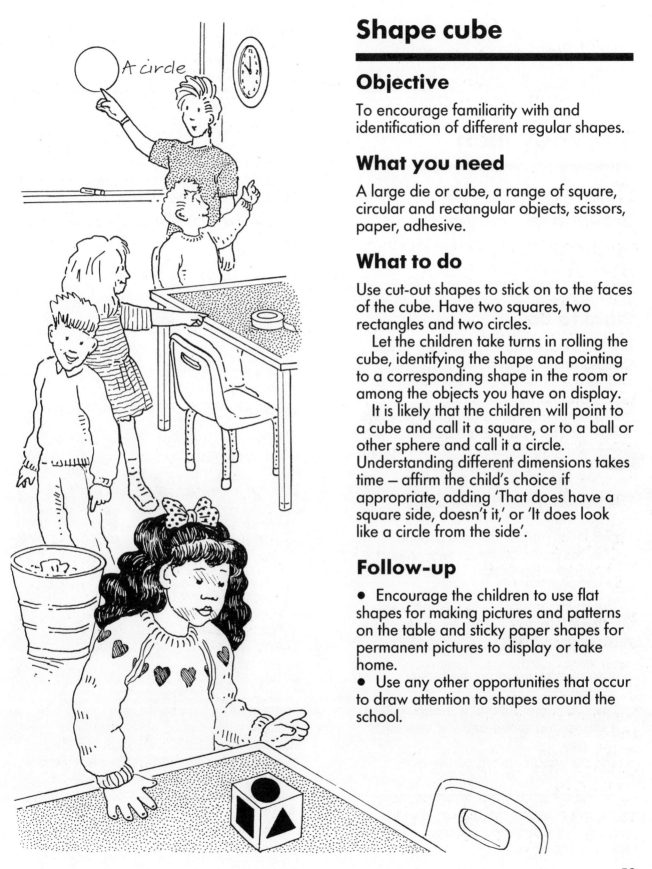

Shape cube

Objective

To encourage familiarity with and identification of different regular shapes.

What you need

A large die or cube, a range of square, circular and rectangular objects, scissors, paper, adhesive.

What to do

Use cut-out shapes to stick on to the faces of the cube. Have two squares, two rectangles and two circles.

Let the children take turns in rolling the cube, identifying the shape and pointing to a corresponding shape in the room or among the objects you have on display.

It is likely that the children will point to a cube and call it a square, or to a ball or other sphere and call it a circle. Understanding different dimensions takes time — affirm the child's choice if appropriate, adding 'That does have a square side, doesn't it,' or 'It does look like a circle from the side'.

Follow-up

• Encourage the children to use flat shapes for making pictures and patterns on the table and sticky paper shapes for permanent pictures to display or take home.
• Use any other opportunities that occur to draw attention to shapes around the school.

The snowman

Objective

To give practice in counting down.

What you need

No special equipment.

What to do

Ask the children to stand in a big circle. Choose one child to stand in the middle and be the snowman, and five more to dance around him. Then sing the following rhyme, while the children in the middle do the appropriate actions. The words will fit to the tune of 'One elephant went out to play' (see page 94).

A snowman stood on the snowy
     ground,
Five little children danced around,
One fell down on the snowy ground –
How many left to dance around? Four!

The rhyme continues in the same way until there are no children left. The last verse goes as follows:

A snowman stood on the snowy
     ground,
The sun came out and it shone around.
It shone and shone and it shone all
     day,
The snowman melted all away.

All the other children can raise their arms and describe the big circle of the sun, while the snowman slowly sinks down to the floor.

Follow-up

• Bring in some ice and let the children watch as it melts.
• Get a chocolate bar and a piece of butter, put them in containers, and leave them in a warm place to melt. Can the children suggest a way of making them go hard again?
• Stick a household candle into Plasticine, put it in a sand tray, light it and supervise the children as they watch the wax melt.

Who is it?

Objective

To encourage observation and to give children an understanding of the process of elimination and sorting.

What you need

No special equipment.

What to do

One child whispers to you the name of another child in the group.

The rest of the class may ask 'yes or no' questions to guess the identity of the mystery child. For example, 'Is it a boy?' 'No.' (All the boys stand to one side.) 'Has she got a dress on?' 'Yes.' (All the girls not wearing dresses stand to one side.) 'Has she got red shoes on?' 'No,' and so on until the identity of the mystery child is discovered.

Follow-up

Give practice in recall by bringing one child to the front and asking the others to describe what he was wearing yesterday. (Sometimes the child you select may have forgotten too!)

Buried treasure

Objective

To encourage directional understanding and knowledge of right and left.

What you need

A little cardboard box or trinket box with a few pretend jewels in it, one left-hand and one right-hand mitten or glove, in different colours.

What to do

Give the odd pair of mittens to one of the children, and point out that the left one is one colour (say yellow) and the right one another colour (say red). Ask the child wearing the mittens to go behind the bookcase or out of sight while the jewels are hidden. When he returns, everyone helps him to find the treasure by giving directions:
- Forwards!
- Right (towards the red mitten)!
- Back!
- Left (towards the yellow mitten)!
- Down!

Repeat the game with another child, with the treasure in a different hiding place.

Follow-up

- Ask the children to give *you* instructions on how to get to the classroom door, the toilets, the playground, the school office and so on.
- Make a table model of a treasure island with papier mâché. Ask the children to make some little boats from everyday materials.

Matching shoes

Objective

To encourage skill in identifying patterns.

What you need

One of each of the children's shoes.

What to do

Put one shoe from each child in the centre of a circle of children sitting with their feet straight out (or nearly so). Let them take turns to take a shoe from the pile and match it to the other one on someone's foot.

Each time they are successful, ask the children how they knew which one was the right match.

This game can be played frequently at first, then at intervals, as young children may have several changes of footwear in one year!

Follow-up

Make some dummy shoes (or use commercial aids) to help the children to practise fastenings. Use laces, Velcro, buckles, buttons and so on.
● Help the children to make a chart of their shoes, grouping them by colours or fastenings.
● Ask the children to draw around a pair of shoes and show the right and left shoes together.
● Make shoe prints on sugar or kitchen paper and look at the patterns on the soles. Which soles do the children think will grip the best in icy weather? Try sliding the shoes down from the top of a ramp or PE slide.

Science skills and understanding

Chapter six

The topic of investigating ourselves and our world could almost encompass the whole of the curriculum! Games can give opportunities to observe using the senses, encouraging the children to look with enquiring eyes at trees, the weather, colours and forces. An enquiring mind is a questioning and reasoning mind — and all of these skills can be enhanced by playing games. Children will use games to explore ideas and relate their own experiences to the other phenomena they observe.

Look, look!

Objective

To encourage observation and understanding of colour and shape.

What you need

Ordinary or chosen objects around the room which are visible to the children.

What to do

This game is a variation of 'I spy'. Say the rhyme below, changing the attributes you ask the children to look for each time.

Look, look!
Look and see.
Point to something . . . YELLOW
When I count to three.
1 . . . 2 . . . 3!

Look, look!
Look and see.
Point to something . . . ROUND
When I count to three.
1 . . . 2 . . . 3!

Play the game several times before inviting a child to choose the colour or shape to look for. Play it on different days with other objects on view.

If all the children point to the same (correct) object, try using constraints to make them look further afield, by excluding 'the yellow door' or 'the round clock'.

Follow-up

Reinforce the children's sense of identity by using the rhyme with their names, changing 'Point to' to 'Wave at'. For example:

Look, look!
Look and see,
Wave at . . . Minnie
When I count to three.
1 . . . 2 . . . 3!

Encourage the children to wait until you say 'three'!

Listen, listen!

Objective

To encourage skill in listening.

What you need

Objects that produce a sound, such as a baby's rattle, a bell, a box of lentils, a plastic bottle half-full of water, a bicycle horn, claves and a tambourine; a large box for the objects; a small screen made from two chairs with a blanket draped over the backs (optional).

What to do

Let the children see you put four or five named objects into the box. Say the rhyme, and then use one of the objects to make a sound.

Listen, listen!
A sound is near,
Listen, listen!
What can you hear?

See if the children can guess which of the objects made the noise, and then play the game again with children making the sounds by rattling the objects.

Next, put some objects into the box without them being seen. Use these objects to make sounds. What do the sounds remind the children of? Where have they heard a sound like that before?

Follow-up

Let the children help you to make a tape recording of different sounds, and leave it for them to listen to again, or invite class visitors to identify the sounds.

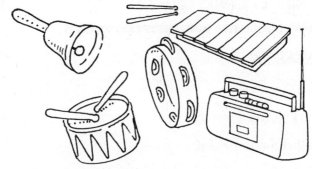

Touch, touch!

Objective

To help children identify and give them confidence in naming parts of the body.

What you need

No special equipment.

What to do

Ask the children to join in with the rhyme and touch their nose, mouth, and so on when you do.

Touch, touch!
Just like me,
Touch your nose
When I count to three.
1 . . . 2 . . . 3!

Encourage them to wait for the 'three!', whilst acknowledging that they have the right idea.

Follow-up

• Make paintings of the children, including one or two life-size ones, and put labels on the parts of the body.
• Draw an outline face and some separate features, each with a number from one to six. Let the children throw a die to determine which feature they can add to the face. The person who completes the face is the winner.

What's changed?

Objective

To encourage observing skills.

What you need

No special equipment.

What to do

When all the children are sitting, take one aside out of view and change something about his appearance. For example, you could roll up one cuff, fold down one sock, undo some buttons or tuck in a pocket flap.

These may appear very minor changes, but young children become adept at spotting the differences, even to a loose shoelace! They will also become better at observing the child before as well as after the change.

Follow-up

Give individual and public praise to children who are learning to put their clothes on after PE by themselves, or who have mastered buttons, belts or laces.

What's missing?

Objective

To encourage recall.

What you need

A shopping bag, a tray, a range of familiar objects, such as a book, a paint pot, a fat crayon, a cup, a mitten, scissors, a roll of sticky tape, a toy car.

What to do

Depending on the age of the children put five to eight objects on the tray, clearly separated.

Ask the children to look at them carefully and remember them. If the children are younger, lift each object up and say its name.

Then turn your back and remove one of the objects secretly into the shopping bag. Show the children the tray again. Let them call out (or ask individuals) what is missing. Repeat the game, removing different objects.

Follow-up

• Reverse the game and add different objects to the tray. Can the children spot the new addition?

• Make a daily 'look and recall' game with a set of objects left in a sorting ring near the classroom door. Remind the children to look at the objects on the way out in the afternoon. Remove one and ask them the following morning what is missing.

• Talk about ways of looking after the children's changing clothes, book-folders and so on so that *they* don't go missing!

Guess the shape

Objective

To encourage children to use their eyes and sense of touch.

What you need

A variety of objects of different shapes, for example, a ball, a shoebox, a large tin, a saucepan; a shopping bag; a small, *thin* piece of sheet.

What to do

Ask the children to cover their eyes while you put an object under the sheet in the middle of the ring. If the children are very young, let them see the group of chosen objects; if they are older keep the objects hidden in a large shopping bag.

It is difficult for the children not to peep while you are hiding the object, but if they do, simply stop and say you have to start again with another object. Most children understand that the game is lost if they peep. If they persist, suggest that they turn their backs as well as covering their eyes, to help them not to see.

When the sheet is in position over the top, let the children guess what the object is. Let one child feel the object, too, to confirm the guess, and then lift off the sheet to show it. Ask the children how they guessed what the object was.

Follow-up

- Try putting two objects close together under the sheet. Can the children guess what they are now?
- Try the same thing putting the objects in unfamiliar positions — the saucepan upside-down, the tin on its side, and so on.

- Draw the children's silhouettes using a strong light to give a clear outline. Draw their shapes on black sugar paper, and let them cut them out and mount them on white paper.

Colour cube

Objective

To encourage awareness and identification of colours.

What you need

A large die or cube, various objects of different colours, coloured paper or paints.

What to do

Make a 'colour cube' from a wooden block or a large die, or make the net of a cube from cardboard. Paint or stick patches of different colours on to the six sides, so that you have red on one side, green on another, and so on.

Let the children take turns to roll the die and name the colour which is uppermost. Then they can point to another object that colour in the room.

Follow-up

- Supply each easel or painting space with one or two colours only. When mounted, the children's paintings could have captions emphasising the colour(s) used: 'Jason painted a red house'; 'Isabel painted a blue cat', and so on.
- Set up a display using just one colour, and change the colour each week or two.

Baby animals

Objective

To link baby animals to their parents.

What you need

No special equipment.

What to do

Say the following rhyme with the children.

The hen has a chicken,
What does it say?
Cheep, cheep, cheep, cheep!
All through the day.

You can easily supply more verses, using the ideas below:
- duck – duckling – quack;
- sheep – lamb – baa;
- pig – piglet – squeal;
- dog – puppy – ruff;
- cow – calf – moo;
- horse – foal – neigh.

Finish the rhyme with this verse:

The snail has a baby,
What does it say?
It doesn't say anything
All through the day.

Follow-up

● Use a jigsaw or commercial game linking animal babies with their parents, or make one with pictures on cards. How do the children recognise which ones are the baby animals? What are human babies like?
● Make a montage of photographs of the children when they were babies. Can they, or any visitors to the classroom, guess which one is which?

I hear thunder

Objective

To give children familiarity with weather signs.

What you need

No special equipment.

What to do

Sing the following rhyme through with the children.

I hear thunder
I hear thunder
Hark, don't you?
Hark, don't you?
Pitter, patter, raindrops
Pitter, patter, raindrops
I'm wet through
So are you.

I see blue skies
I see blue skies
Way up high
Way up high
Out into the sunshine
Out into the sunshine
We'll soon dry
We'll soon dry.

The second time you sing this through, add some sound effects and actions. Encourage the children to clap their hands for thunder, drum on the floor with their fingers for the rain, sweep their arms in a wide circle for the blue skies, and draw a big circle in the air for the sun.

Follow-up

• Try accompanying the song with percussion. Use drums or cymbals for the thunder, claves or rattles for the rain, chime bars for the blue sky and . . . what would the children suggest for the sunshine? How would they represent lightning? Or snow?

• In movement lessons try showing different kinds of weather by different kinds of movement, both on the spot and around the room.

• Make puppet weather characters by mounting cardboard people on lolly sticks. Give each one the characteristics of a particular sort of weather, making sure the cloudy character is fun too. Select the ones relevant to each day and stand them up in a Plasticine base.

Brainstorming

Objective

To gain an insight into some of the children's experiences and associations.

What you need

No special equipment.

What to do

Choose a topic that you are about to introduce to the children, or a subject with which they are already familiar. Suitable subjects might include:
• water;
• food;
• grannies;
• babies;
• shops;
• mountains;
• fire.

When the children are all together, ask them to tell you *anything* they know about that subject. Support them with examples at first; for example, 'When I turn the taps on, water comes out . . .'; 'I wash my hands with water . . .'.

This may give you a kind of class concept-map, and an idea about which objects will have interest and meaning for the children, such as, in the case of water, a watering-can, an umbrella, and so on. A collection of these things provides first-hand materials for science investigations.

Elephants can fly!

Objective

To encourage listening, responding and classification skills.

What you need

No special equipment.

What to do

Ask the children to stand in a space. Tell them that you are going to call out sentences like, 'Birds can fly!' The children should raise their arms and pretend to flap their wings whenever they hear you mention birds or any other flying thing, such as ducks, bees and aeroplanes, but every so often you will call out 'Elephants can fly!', or pigs, or dogs, or houses . . . When you do this, the children should keep their arms down. Those caught out can sit down until a new game begins.

Depending on the age of the children, speak fairly fast and put non-flying objects in fairly often. You can either use repeated familiar objects or vary the list.

69

Follow-up

- Discuss the things that fly and how they are made. Make paper aeroplanes and spinners.
- Let the children blow bubbles outside and watch them float away.
- Put up pictures of the most regular bird visitors to the playground, together with their names to encourage identification. If it is winter, put out food for the birds.
- Read a story about Dumbo — the elephant who *could* fly!

Suction

Objective

To make children aware of the force of air pressure.

What you need

Straws, dried peas and/or empty pistachio nut shells, pieces of paper, a sand-timer (optional).

What to do

Divide the children into manageable groups, and give them straws and pieces of paper. Ask them to put one end of the straw near the paper and suck the other end. What happens? What are they sucking into their mouths?

Give them a pile of peas and/or nut shells and ask if they can transfer them from the pile to the paper. Older children could race against time using a sand-timer.

Follow-up

- Show the children a vacuum cleaner and spread more dried peas and nut shells on the floor. Then switch on the vacuum cleaner, and let them listen to the sound, feel the suction effect on their hands and the air expelled at the other end. Finally, let the children sweep up the peas and nut shells using the vacuum cleaner.
- Use everyday materials to make models of vacuum cleaners — upright or cylinder.

Little red wagon

Objective

To give children familiarity with vehicle parts and names.

What you need

No special equipment.

What to do

Ask the children to sit, and then sing this song to the tune of 'In and out the dusty bluebells' (see page 94).

Jogging up and down in my little red
    wagon
Jogging up and down in my little red
    wagon
Jogging up and down in my little red
    wagon
Won't you be my darling?

Oh, what's happened to the little red wagon? (× 3)
Won't you be my darling?

One wheel's off and the axle's dragging . . .

Mary's got a hammer and she will fix it . . .

Have another ride in the little red wagon . . .

Oh, what's happened to the little red wagon? . . .

Another wheel's off and the bonnet's broken . . .

Johnny's got a spanner and he will fix it . . .

Have another ride in the little red wagon . . .

You can continue to have things break off the little red wagon until you or the children are fed up, but be warned – some children could go on for ever! During the 'jogging along' verses, the children can bounce up and down on their bottoms. During the 'Oh, what's happened' verses, express surprise with your eyes and hands, and in the 'fix it' verses, either the named child or everyone can pretend to use the tool to fix the wagon.

Follow-up

- Provide toys and construction kits that require fastening together, preferably with big nuts and bolts.
- Make a little red wagon with grocery boxes to fit two children.

Consequences

Objective

To encourage reasoning skills and the ability to use language appropriately.

What you need

No special equipment.

What to do

Offer the children the start of a sentence for them to conclude. They will need examples from you to get the idea at first, so give them the beginning, pause, then offer one or two suggestions, requesting theirs. Encourage many answers.
- I got very cold because . . .
- I got very hot because . . .
- I felt really hungry so I . . .
- I felt really thirsty so I . . .
- The light wouldn't come on because . . .
- We couldn't open the door because . . .
- I couldn't lift the box because . . .
- If you switch on the cooker it . . .
- If you run down the corridor somebody might . . .
- We didn't get wet in the rain because . . .

Accept all the children's suggestions. You might follow some with the question, 'Why do you think that?'

Oats and beans and barley grow

Objective

To introduce the idea of cereal crops and encourage classification skills.

What you need

No special equipment.

What to do

Say the following rhyme with the children, doing the actions:

Oats and beans and barley grow
　　[hands rising upwards]
Oats and beans and barley grow
Nor you, nor I, nor anyone knows
　　[shake head]
How oats and beans and barley grow.
　　[hands rising upwards]

First the farmer sows the seed
　　[wide gestures as if scattering seed]
Then he stands and takes his ease
　　[hands on hips]
Stamps his feet and claps his hands
And turns around to view the land.
　　[turn round with hand shading eyes]

Do you want a partner?
Do you want a partner?
For if you do
You must be true
And choose him very shortly.
　　[form pairs and dance round in a circle]

Follow-up

• Make a collection of breakfast cereals for the children to investigate, and chart their preferences.

• Visit a nearby farm or show the children some information books to find out about present-day methods of sowing seeds.
• Read the story of the *Little Red Hen*. There are various versions of this well-known story, including one in the Ladybird series.

Pancake

Objective

To use a rhyme in a topical context.

What you need

No special equipment.

What to do

This is a good poem to use on or near Pancake Day (Shrove Tuesday). Show the children how to do the appropriate stirring, shaking and tossing actions to go with the words.

Mix a pancake,
Stir a pancake,
Pop it in the pan.
Fry the pancake,
Toss the pancake,
Catch if if you can.

Follow-up

• Cook some pancakes while the children watch, and give them some to taste.
• Play tossing and catching games with beanbags in a big room or outside.

Sound and music

Chapter seven

Hearing is a wonderful sense, and exploring it can be novel, exciting, and even scary at times. Music is one of life's great pleasures, and introducing children to its magic early on gives them access to a resource which is never far away.

Rhyme and rhythm are expressed by the hands and the body, and listening, interpreting and responding skills can all be developed through games. Singing and dancing with others is a shared delight. It isn't important whether you think you have a singing voice or not – just sing anyway! The pleasure is in sharing the song.

Musical statues

Objective

To encourage children to listen and respond to music.

What you need

A tape-recorder and musical tapes.

What to do

While you play a tape of music, the children can skip and dance around. When the music stops they must stand very still. Children who move must sit down, and the game goes on. It is important not to repeat the game too many times before giving the children who are sitting out the opportunity to stand up and dance again.

Follow-up

Play some music that illustrates a particular mood, or the weather or the seasons. For example, you could use the storm scene from Beethoven's *Pastoral Symphony*, excerpts from Holst's *The Planets Suite*, Vivaldi's *Four Seasons*, Strauss waltzes, snatches of jazz and blues, and so on. Let the children listen with their eyes closed. What does the music remind them of? You could choose one piece to dramatise with the children.

Hum the tune

Objective

To help children to listen carefully to tunes.

What you need

A list of well-known tunes, an instrument (optional).

What to do

Hum a nursery rhyme or song known to the children, accompanying yourself on an instrument if you have one. Perfect pitch is not necessary — just *sing*! Remember, when starting off, to think of a note, then think of a higher one. Suitable songs might include:
- Ring a ring o' roses;
- Pop goes the weasel;
- Humpty Dumpty;
- Hot cross buns;
- Row, row, row your boat;
- The grand old Duke of York;
- Three blind mice;
- Jack and Jill;
- See-saw, Marjorie Daw;
- Sing a song of sixpence.

Follow-up

• Can the children guess the tune if you hum only the first one or two lines?
• Use chime bars or a xylophone to play the notes of a familiar tune.
• Ask the children if they can make up tunes with the instruments, or invent rhythms for everyone to copy.

Clap, clap

Objective

To help engage or maintain children's attention.

What you need

No special equipment.

What to do

Use this game for quietening the children, or for getting everyone involved. Start the rhythmic beat by clapping, and intersperse each different movement with two claps, all done fairly quickly. For example:

Clap, clap
Clap, clap
Clap, clap
Clap, clap
Tap your knee
Clap, clap
Tap your shoulder
Clap, clap
Tap your nose
Clap, clap
Tap your . . .

Younger children could do the different movements twice:

Tap your knee
Clap, clap
Tap your knee
Clap, clap

Follow-up

This game could be played in the hall before assembly to engage all the children's attention. Follow it up with 'Follow my leader' (see page 76).

Follow my leader

Objective

To develop children's sense of rhythm and help improve their concentration.

What you need

No special equipment.

What to do

Begin to clap a simple rhythm, encouraging the children to follow suit. When your first rhythm is established, change it, and keep on changing the rhythms as the children learn them.

In the following examples, X represents one clap, — a rest, and xx two little claps.

- X X X X|X X X X|X X X X|

- X X X–|X X X–| and

- X–X–|X–X–|X–X–|

- xx X X X|xx X X X|xx X X X|

- X xx X X|X xx X X| and

- X X–xx|X X–xx|

This can be a useful game to play when you are waiting for the children to settle down. Start the first rhythm without speaking, nodding to those children with whom you have eye-contact to join in, and continue that rhythm until everyone joins in without you having to speak.

Use the same technique to reinforce the rhythm of a new song you are teaching; for example:

Little don-key; | Little don-key
xx   X – X | xx   X – X

On the dus-ty |road
xx   X – X |X –

Follow-up

Ask if any child would like to start a rhythm off. It doesn't matter if you have had that rhythm before; the change is that the child takes responsibility for initiating the rhythm.

Where's the bell?

Objective

To encourage listening and directional skills.

What you need

A little bell, or similar.

What to do

The children should all stand in a ring with their hands behind their backs. Ask one child to go behind a screen or bookcase while the bell is given to one of the children in the ring. The child who has hidden then returns to the middle of the circle and tries to guess who has the bell by listening for its occasional ringing. The child in the middle should continue to guess until the bell is discovered.

Young children will use their eyes to help them guess too, by watching who is moving. Older children could perhaps guess by listening with their eyes closed.

Follow-up

• Encourage the children to listen to sounds travelling in different ways; for example, let them listen to a pencil tapping on the table, then listen to the same sound with one ear resting on the table.
• Blow up a balloon and let the children take turns to speak through it. One child should have his ear against the balloon, while the other puts his mouth up close to it.
• Ask the children to talk into cupped hands and containers and listen to the sound.

The bunnies

Objective

To use a singing game to have fun.

What you need

No special equipment.

What to do

Choose some children to be the bunnies lying in the corner asleep. The others can gather nearby and sing the song below. At 'hop' the bunnies get up and do nine hops. The groups can then change round.

See the little bunnies fast asleep!
Do you think we'll wake them if we
peep?
Little bunny, are you ill,
That you lie so quiet and still?
Hop, hop, hop.
Hop, hop, hop.
HOP! HOP! HOP!

The first four lines can be sung to the tune of 'Five currant buns'. The hops can be sung 'soh, doh, doh; te, ray, ray; me, ray, doh'.

Follow-up

• Rabbits hop using all four feet, but we hop on one. Let the children hop like rabbits, crouching down and doing bunny-hops on to their hands, kicking their toes up at the back.
• Practise ordinary hopping on mats, and hopping from one foot to the other.
• Find a tape or record with music to hop to.
• Read 'Hoppity' by A. A. Milne from *When We Were Very Young* (Methuen).

Ride a cock horse

Objective

To encourage movement to music.

What you need

Percussion instruments with bell-like sounds, such as the sides of tambourines, bells, rattles and chime bars.

What to do

Split the children into two groups — one to gallop around, and the other to be musicians. Then sing the following rhyme together:

> Ride a cock horse
> To Banbury Cross
> To see a fine lady
> Upon a white horse;
> Rings on her fingers
> And bells on her toes,
> She shall have music
> Wherever she goes.

During the first half of this rhyme, the children can gallop (carefully) around. In the second half, the musicians can join in to accompany the others. Repeat the rhyme, and then let the groups change around.

Follow-up

• Ask the children where we can hear ringing and bells. The playtime bell? The telephone? The doorbell?
• Make some fairy bells with clean milk-bottle tops, threaded through with string and fastened together on an old paint brush, lolly stick or other stick.
• Play 'Where's the bell?' (see page 77).

Mrs Macaroni

Objective

To give children a chance to enjoy rhythm in a group game.

What you need

No special equipment.

What to do

Ask the children to sit or stand in a circle while a chosen child trots around in the centre. Sing the following rhyme to the tune of 'Bobby Shaftoe'.

> Here comes Mrs Macaroni
> Riding on her snow white pony
> Here she comes in all her glory
> Mrs Macaroni.
>
> Pom, pom Susianna
> Pom, pom Susianna
> Pom, pom Susianna
> Mrs Macaroni.

During the second verse the children can clap in time to the rhythm, or march around in their circle. Repeat the game with a different child as Mrs Macaroni.

Follow-up

• Bring in a variety of pasta for the children to look at, including shells, macaroni and butterflies. Let them look at the shapes, feel them and try crushing them.
• If you have enough, use some of the pasta for making macaroni cheese.
• Dye some of the pasta pieces with strong inks, paints or food colourings and let the children use them for collages.

The grand old Duke of York

Objective

To help children feel the rhythm of marching.

What you need

Drums, claves, kazoos.

What to do

Choose one child to be the Duke, and designate areas to be the top and bottom of the hill, for example the door and the further wall. Split the children into two groups, one with percussion instruments and the other to be soldiers.

The musicians can remain seated and beat time while the remaining children march behind the Duke. They should end up in the middle of the room.

The grand old duke of York,
He had ten thousand men,
He marched them up to the top of the hill
And he marched them down again.
And when they were up, they were up.
And when they were down, they were down.
And when they were only half-way up,
They were neither up nor down.

Repeat the rhyme, swapping the groups around and choosing a different Duke.

Follow-up

Read the poems 'Half-way down', 'Buckingham Palace' and 'At home' in *When We Were Very Young* by A. A. Milne (Methuen).

Car wash

Objective

To give children an opportunity to enjoy sounds.

What you need

No special equipment.

What to do

Have two lines of children facing each other, and choose one child to be the car to be washed. The two lines of children will be the rollers in the automatic car wash. They can do the actions suggested in the rhyme, and supply the appropriate sound effects!

Here comes the car
All dirty and grey
   [the 'car' approaches the lines of children]
Here comes the car
To be washed today.

The car will be clean
As quick as a wink
Money in the machine
   [the 'car' pretends to put coins in a slot]
Goes clink, clink, clink.

Here go the rollers
Splosh, splosh, splosh
   *[the 'rollers' pretend to wash the 'car' as s/he
   goes down the line]*
Giving the car
A lovely wash.

Water on the windows
Pitter, pitter, patter
   *[the 'rollers' pat the 'car' and pretend to work up
   a lather]*
Soap all over,
Slither, slither, slather.

Rollers rolling
Birra, birra, brush
Car's all clean now
It's had its wash.
   [the 'car' emerges from the end of the line]

Repeat the rhyme, with another child in the car wash.

Follow-up

• Use grocery boxes to make model cars. Put them in an area labelled 'Car sales' and let the children point out the workings, design and good points to prospective customers. Put large price labels on the cars.
• Make a model car wash either for these box cars or small toy ones.

Weaving a garland

Objective

To encourage singing and turn-taking.

What you need

No special equipment.

What to do

The children stand in a ring holding hands. Choose one child to begin the garland, and sing the tune through once (see page 95). On repeating the tune, the chosen child drops her partners' hands and crosses her hands over before joining on again (like in 'Auld Lang Syne'). Then at the start of each line the next child on her right or left does the same, until all the children are woven in.

Come, let's weave a garland,
I'll show you how it's done,
It's started by Lisa,
Then we join in one by one.
We must cross hands just like she does,
Oh, won't it be fun!

Follow-up

• Make or buy some sewing cards for the children to use with thick needles and wool. The children can use these cards to sew numbers, letters, picture outlines or simply to give them practice in the skill of sewing.
• Show the children how to make 'samplers' using squares of coloured open-weave fabric and criss-cross line sewing.
• Make a collection of different fabrics and look with the children at the different colours, patterns and weaves.

Lavender's blue

Objective

To use a traditional rhyme to encourage a sense of rhythm.

What you need

No special equipment.

What to do

Help the children to learn the first verse. Then encourage them to clap out the rhythm while singing it. (This needs to be done slowly at first to allow the children to clap the syllables of 'dilly, dilly'.)

Practise this a few times. Then clap out the rhythm without singing it, stopping somewhere at random. Can the children guess where you have got up to?

Lavender's blue
Dilly, dilly
Lavender's green,
When you are king
Dilly, dilly
I will be queen.

Call up your men
Dilly, dilly
Come to the farm,
Some feed the hens
Dilly, dilly
There in the barn.

Some to make hay
Dilly, dilly
Some to cut corn,
While you and I
Dilly, dilly
Keep ourselves warm.

Lavender's green
Dilly, dilly
Lavender's blue
If you love me
Dilly, dilly
I will love you.

Follow-up

● Use percussion instruments or tap the floor to accompany the song.
● Choose some children to be dancers, and others to play percussion instruments in the 'orchestra'. Arrange the dancers in two lines, with boys facing girls. Then while the musicians play their instruments, the dancers can move as follows:

Lavender's blue
Dilly, dilly
[boys step forward and bow]
Lavender's green
[girls step forward and curtsey]
When I am king
[boys step and bow]
Dilly, dilly
I shall be queen.
[girls step and curtsey]

In this version, the boys and girls take it in turn to sing the lines, so that the boys sing while they step forward, and then the girls sing and move.

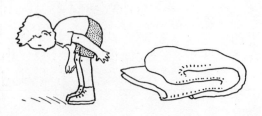

Imagination and drama

Chapter eight

Children from three to six are moving from the dramatic spontaneity of early play to a deeper understanding of themselves in relation to the rest of the world. Fantasy, imagination and memory can be used in structured role-play to explore unfamiliar situations or experiences, such as visits from the doctor. Imagination can be used to help children to recall characteristics of objects and phenomena and to symbolise them in active play. It can also help children learn to abstract the property from the object. Games can help them to use their hands and their bodies to communicate in free and controlled ways.

Can you walk on tiptoe?

Objective

To encourage the children's exploration of the qualities of movement.

What you need

No special equipment.

What to do

Say the following rhyme together, doing the actions suggested by the words.

> Can you walk on tiptoe,
> As softly as a cat?
> Can you stamp along the road,
> JUST LIKE THAT?
> Can you take some great big strides,
> Just like a giant can?
> Or walk along so slowly
> Like a little old man?
>
> Can you jump out of the pond
> Just like a little frog?
> Can you wag your busy tail
> Just like a friendly dog?
> Can you slither like a snake
> Moving on the ground?
> Can you roll up very tight
> Like a hedgehog small and round?

Follow-up

Use one or more percussion instruments, suggested by the children, to accompany the movements.

The wind

Objective

To let children experience different movements and think about the nature of trees.

What you need

No special equipment.

What to do

Say the following rhyme, and encourage the children to move as appropriate for the different trees.

> Oak trees stand fast
> When the wind blows past.
>
> Willow branches sway
> When the wind blows their way.
>
> Pine trees reach high
> When the wind blows by.
>
> And we run and play
> When the wind blows our way.

The children could spread out their arms and stand still and rigid to represent the oak, droop their arms and swing them gently from side to side for the willow, reach their arms up high for the pine, and in the last verse they could run, skip and hop around the room, until you give the call to stop.

84

Pass the object

Objective

To develop the children's imagination.

What you need

No special equipment.

What to do

Sit with the children in a ring and imagine that you are holding an object in your hands or arms. Let your actions indicate what the object might be, for example by stroking an imaginary rabbit or cat. Then pretend to pass it on to the next child, and so on round the ring. You could ask the children to say what they think the object might be. More than one object may correspond to the action. Encourage imaginative responses by asking, 'What else could it be?'

Some ideas for imaginary objects include:
- a full cup;
- a mirror;
- a baby;
- a bag of sweets;
- something sticky;
- a flower;
- a heavy weight;
- a dandelion clock;
- a drink carton and straw;
- a pin.

Follow-up

Bring some real objects to hold and pass around the ring, with the intention of looking at how we hold them, where we support them, and why we need to use caution. Consider safety aspects — whether because of the danger of damaging the object or the risk of hurting oneself or others.

Snow

Objective

To encourage children to move at different speeds, and to stretch their imaginations.

What you need

No special equipment.

What to do

The children can play this game seated, using their hands and arms only, or standing in a space and using their whole bodies. Say the rhyme together, and encourage the children to move at different speeds as appropriate for each verse, coming slowly to rest in the last verse.

Ally ally owing
Snow snow snowing,

Ally ally aster
Snow snow faster,

Ally ally ower
Snow snow slower,

Ally ally op
Snow snow stop.

Follow-up

- Do other movement activities based on different sorts of weather, such as wind, rain, sunshine and shadows.
- Ask the children to paint pictures using only white paint.
- Bring some ice into the classroom to look at; or if the weather is suitable, take the children out to explore the qualities of the snow.

A farmer went trotting

Objective

To help children move to rhythm.

What you need

No special equipment.

What to do

Ask the children to sit in a comfortable area, and say this rhyme together. At each 'bumpety, bumpety, bump' or 'lumpety, lumpety, lump', they should bounce their bottoms up and down on the floor.

A farmer went trotting upon his grey
    mare,
Bumpety, bumpety, bump,
With his daughter beside him, so rosy
    and fair,
Lumpety, lumpety, lump.

A raven cried 'Croak' and they all
    tumbled down,
Bumpety, bumpety, bump,
The mare broke her knees and the
    farmer his crown,
Lumpety, lumpety, lump.

The mischievous raven flew laughing
    away,
Bumpety, bumpety, bump,
And swore he would serve them the
    same the next day,
Lumpety, lumpety, lump.

Explain to the children any vocabulary that might be confusing.

Follow-up

Use everyday materials and Plasticine or use a commercially produced farm set for play and discussion.

Are you there, Mr Bear?

Objective

To encourage quick responses.

What you need

No special equipment.

What to do

Choose one child to be the bear in the den. The other children can either stay seated or stand up and walk towards the bear.

Bear: Knock! Knock!
Children: Who's there?
          Is it you, Mr Bear?

If the bear then imitates another animal ('Miaow, miaow'; 'Woof, woof', etc.) the children must copy her. If she growls, the children either crouch right down if they are sitting, or run back to their places and sit down quickly before the bear finishes growling.

Follow-up

- Sing 'The Teddy Bears' Picnic'.
- Paint pictures of big, brown bears.
- Make a collection of teddy bears. Put them in order from biggest to smallest.
- Play 'What's the time, Mr Wolf?'

The animals' fair

Objective

To help children identify the different ways in which we and other animals move.

What you need

No special equipment.

What to do

Stand with the children in a ring, and pick one child to stand in the centre and be the elephant. During the second verse the elephant can move around heavily, stamping his feet and swinging his trunk; during the third verse everyone can copy him.

> I went to the animals' fair
> The birds and the beasts were there,
> And guess what I could see?
> An elephant following me.
>
> And he went . . .
> Thump, thump,
> Thump, thump,
> Thump, thump,
> Thump.
>
> So we went . . .
> Thump, thump,
> Thump, thump,
> Thump, thump,
> Thump.

Make up some other verses based on other animals — for example, you could have a horse going 'clip-clop', a rabbit going 'jump, jump', a tortoise going 'crawl, crawl', and so on. Let the children suggest other animals and their movements, and let them take turns to go in the middle and demonstrate.

Follow-up

• Make a display of story and information books about animals.
• Encourage the children to paint pictures of animals, drawing attention to their feet and legs.

There was a princess long ago

Objective

To help children recall a story and dramatise it simply.

What you need

No special equipment.

What to do

Choose one child to be the princess, who stands in the middle of the ring. Ask two other children to be the witch and the prince. Then sing the following rhyme with the children, and do the actions. The tune is on page 95.

There was a princess long ago,
Long ago, long ago.
There was a princess long ago,
Long, long ago.

And she lived in a tall dark tower
  [children raise their arms up]
Tall dark tower, tall dark tower,
And she lived in a tall dark tower,
Long, long ago.

A wicked witch she cast a spell . . .
  [the witch pretends to put a spell on the princess, who falls asleep]

A great big forest grew around . . .
  [the children link arms at the elbow and raise their hands]

A handsome prince came riding by . . .
  [the prince rides around the outside of the ring]

He cut the branches with his sword . . .
  [pretends to chop at the branches and the children drop their arms]

He took the princess by the hand . . .
  [goes to the princess and wakes her up]

And everybody's happy now . . .
  [all the children take a partner and dance around the room]

Follow-up

● Draw round some of the children to provide shapes for them to paint or cover in collage and make a large mural of the fairy story. The castle could be covered in shiny foil paper and then partly obscured with trees made from florists' sticks and tissue paper, interlaced with green garden twine.
● This action rhyme also makes a good activity for showing to parents or at assembly.

Miss Polly

Objective

To give children experience of sequencing events.

What you need

No special equipment.

What to do

Say the following rhyme together, doing the actions.

Miss Polly had a dolly
Who was sick, sick, sick.
   [pretend to hold baby]
So she called to the doctor
   [pretend to telephone]
To come quick, quick, quick.

The doctor came
With his bag and his hat,
   [mime holding bag and lifting hat]
And he knocked at the door
With a rat-a-tat-tat.
   [knock]

He looked at the dolly
And he shook his head,
   [shake head]
And he said, 'Miss Polly
Put him straight to bed'.
   [wag finger]

Then he wrote on a paper
For a pill, pill, pill
   [pretend to write]
'I'll be back in the morning
When he's well, well, well.'
   [wave and smile]

Traditionally the last line is 'With my bill, bill, bill', but this is not always meaningful to children.

Follow-up

● Ask the children if they have been to the doctor's and what happened. Is their doctor a man or a woman? Did she listen to or feel their throat or tap their chest? What do they think she did that for?
● Turn the home corner into a clinic or doctor's waiting room and surgery. Supply white shirts with cut-off sleeves or white cleaning jackets for the doctor and nurse. Leave a scribble pad and pencils for the children to write their prescriptions.

I had a little pony

Objective

To encourage children to think about caring for animals.

What you need

No special equipment.

What to do

Choose three children to be the pony, the pony's owner and the lady. Ask the others to sit in a ring, and the three can stand in the middle. Then say the following rhyme together:

I had a little pony,
His name was Dapple Grey.
I lent him to a lady
To ride a mile away.
She whipped him,
She beat him,
She rode him through the mire!
I would not lend my pony now
For all a lady's hire.

While you say the rhyme, the owner can pretend to give the pony to the lady. The lady then follows the galloping pony around the ring pretending to whip and beat him. The owner stops the pony and takes him away, stroking him.

When they have finished, everyone can clap the three children. Repeat the rhyme with other children taking the parts.

Follow-up

• Ask the children what the pony in the rhyme would feel like. What would the owner feel like? Why do the children think the lady behaved like that?
• Talk about caring for animals at home and why so many people like to keep pets. Make sets to show the animals the children keep and love.

Six little ducks

Objective

To give children a chance to enjoy movement.

What you need

No special equipment.

What to do

Sing the following song together, and do the actions. The music is on page 96.

Six little ducks that I once knew
Fat ones, skinny ones, they were too,
   [use arms to show 'fat' and 'skinny']
But one little duck
With feathers on his back,
   *[hand behind back, fingers moving to show
   feathers]*
He ruled the others
   [wag finger]
With a 'Quack, quack, quack!'
   [flap elbows]
He ruled the others
   [wag finger]
With a 'Quack, quack, quack.'
   [flap elbows]

Down to the river they would go
Wibble, wobble, wibble, wobble, to
   and fro.
   [sway from side to side]
But one little duck
With feathers on his back,
He ruled . . .

Home from the river they would go
Wibble, wobble, wibble, wobble, to
   and fro . . .

Follow-up

• Find some posters or books with pictures of ducks. Ask the children what kind of feet the ducks have. Are they the same as ours? What do they use their feet for? Which is easier for ducks — walking or swimming? Which is easier for us? Why?

• During water play with older children, ask them to try dipping their hands into the water, one hand covered with baby oil. What do they notice?

Here we come on ponies

Objective

To give children an awareness of how animals move.

What you need

No special equipment.

What to do

Let the children trot round the room as you sing the following rhyme:

   Here we come on ponies,
   Ponies, ponies,
   Here we come on ponies,
   Whoa, whoa, whoa!
      [pretend to pull on reins]
   Stop a moment just to say
   'How do you do this sunny day?'
      [bow or curtsey]
   We are going to London,
   London, London,
   We are going to London
   This fine day.

Follow-up

Explore the way other animals move. Can the children move like a rabbit? A cat? A mouse? A snail? A caterpillar?

Music

Punchinello

What can you do, Punch - in - el - lo lit - tle fel - low?

What can you do, Punch - in - el - lo lit - tle man?

This way and that way

Did you ev - er see a las - sie go this way and

that way, Did you ev - er see a las - sie go this way and

that, Go this way and that way, go this way and that way, Did you
ev - er see a las - sie go this way and that?

Down by the river

Down by the ri - ver where the green grass grows, There sits Sa - rah
wash - ing her clothes, She sings, she sings, she sings so sweet,
She calls to her play - mate a - cross the street.

Elephants on a string

One el-e-phant went out to play Up-on a piece of string one day. She thought it such tre-men-dous fun She called for an-oth-er el-e-phant to come.

In and out the dusty bluebells

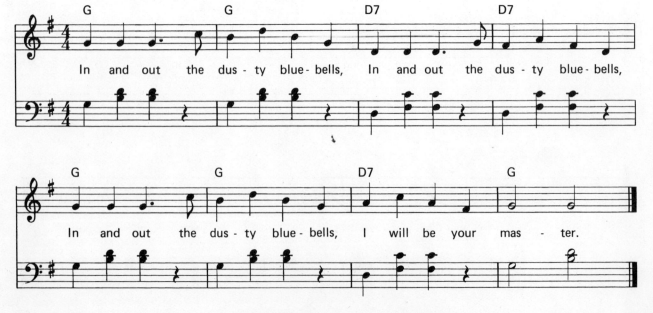

In and out the dus-ty blue-bells, In and out the dus-ty blue-bells, In and out the dus-ty blue-bells, I will be your mas - ter.

Weaving a garland

Come, let's weave a gar-land, I'll show you how it's done, It's start-ed by Li-sa, then we join in one by one, We must cross hands just like she does, Oh won't it be fun!

There was a princess long ago

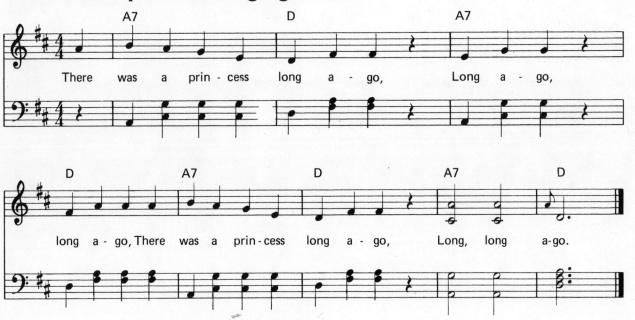

There was a prin-cess long a-go, Long a-go, long a-go, There was a prin-cess long a-go, Long, long a-go.

Six little ducks

Six lit - tle ducks that I once knew, Fat ones, skin - ny ones they were too, But one lit - tle duck with fea - thers on his back, He rul'd the oth - ers with a 'Quack, quack, quack! Quack, quack, quack!' He rul'd the oth - ers with a 'Quack, quack, quack!'